Home-Grown Food

After graduating from Cambridge and th
College of Art, David Wickers has worked
primarily as a freelance writer in various fields,
including TV comedy, children's books, travel and
investigative journalism. He has taught both in
schools and colleges and has travelled widely in
Western and Eastern Europe, North and South
America, West and North Africa and the Middle
East.

What the press said about THE COMPLETE URBAN FARMER by David Wickers

GOOD HOUSEKEEPING Backyard and balcony growing is on the increase, with lots of us trying to cadge every inch of space we can to produce more food, so THE COMPLETE URBAN FARMER by David Wickers is a useful book for town dwellers, with its ideas for growing things indoors and in windowboxes as well as backyards. Nice to give.

WOMAN'S OWN Ever looked in despair at your pocket handkerchief backyard or wilting window-box and longed to join the grow-your-own-veg brigade? Well, now you can. According to a new book, it's not space you need so much as know-how. THE COMPLETE URBAN FARMER, by David Wickers, tells you how to use every inch of the balcony, the bathroom, the office—even under the bed! (Mushrooms aren't fussy about light.) Having sown and grown, Mr Wickers tells you how to store, bottle, cook and pickle your produce.

IDEAL HOME David Wickers has a practical and original approach, and his text is illustrated with very clear line drawings.

COSMOPOLITAN . . . highly original . . . a book for townees who long for a taste of country life. There are plenty of ideas for small gardens, patios and window boxes, too. If beams up the bannisters are your idea of fun, this book is essential reading.

BBC . . . a very practical book this. With the high cost of fruit and vegetables, more and more people are growing their own. But what do you do if you haven't got a large garden — well David Wickers has the answer in his book THE COMPLETE URBAN FARMER — growing your own fruit and vegetables in town.

THE SOIL ASSOCIATION The greatest attraction of this book lies in the masses of imaginative, original and resourceful suggestions for utilising all available space in the house and garden, and every variety of utensil, for the production of food by the townee.

THE OBSERVER . . . a jolly interesting book on how to grow things in small and unexpected spaces, particularly indoors. It tells you how to grow in rotation to achieve two or even three crops a year, and suggests plenty of things you can grow without a garden — herbs (of course), mushrooms, melons, marrows, strawberries, tomatoes, peppers, and aubergines.

David Wickers
HOME-GROWN FOOD

With drawings by Sharon Finmark

Fontana/Collins

First published by Julian Friedmann Publishers Ltd
1977 as *Indoor Farming*
First issued in Fontana 1978

Text copyright © David Wickers 1977
Drawings copyright © Sharon Finmark 1977

Book designed by Dick Vine

Made and printed in Great Britain by
Fletcher & Son Ltd, Norwich

To my parents, with love and thanks

CONTENTS

ACKNOWLEDGEMENTS

The author would like to express his thanks to the following for their kind assistance:

    The National Institute of Agricultural Botany, Cambridge
    Long Ashton Research Station, Bristol
    The Ministry of Agriculture, Fisheries and Food
    Stockbridge House Experimental Horticulture Station, York
    The Electricity Council
    Carters Tested Seeds Ltd, Clwyd
    The United States Department of Agriculture, Washington DC
    Transatlantic Plastics Ltd, Isle of Wight
    Stewart Plastics Ltd, Croydon
    Emblem Engineering Ltd, Surrey
    Thompson and Morgan (Ipswich) Ltd
    Humex Ltd, Surrey
    Phostrogen Ltd, Clwyd
    Properco Ltd (Growpax seeds) Sussex
    The Royal Horticultural Society's Garden, Wisley, Surrey
    Aylesbury College of Further Education, Buckinghamshire
    The National Vegetable Society, Surrey
    John F. Tuey
    Randall B. Thomas
    General Electric Company, Ohio
    The American Horticultural Society, Virginia
    W. Atlee Burpee, California
    Fisons Garden Products, Cambridge
    Autogrow Ltd, Northumberland
    Spencer Bayley Ltd, Hampshire
    New Tomorrow Inc, California
    Sudbury Technical Products, Kent

and also to:

    The Department of Horticulture, University of Illinois, Urbana-Champaign; Mellinger's Inc, Ohio; Earl May Seed and Nursery Co, Iowa; G.W. Park Seed Co. Inc, South Carolina; Duro-Test Corp, New Jersey; Environmental Dynamics, California; Vegetable Factory Inc, New York; Plantabbs, Maryland; House Plant Corner, Maryland; Shoplite Co, New Jersey; Agricultural Research Station, Maryland; New York State College of Agriculture and Life Sciences, New York; Horticultural Research Institute Inc, Washington DC; Harris Seeds, New York; The Sylvania Co, Massachusetts; The Old Rectory Herb Garden, Kent; Cranmore Vineyard, Isle of Wight; LBS Polythene, Lancashire; W.J. Unwin, Cambridgeshire; JSM (Horticulture) Ltd, London; Amateur Tobacco Growers'

Association, London; Merrydown Wine Co. Ltd, Sussex; House Horticultural and Garden Growers' Automation, Barnet; Department of Architecture, Cambridge University; Darmycel (UK) Ltd, Sussex; Angex Ltd, London; International Working Group on Soilless Culture, Wageningen, The Netherlands; Thorn Lighting, London; Agricultural and Horticultural Research Station, University of Bristol; A.E. Canham, Department of Agriculture and Horticulture, University of Reading; The Soil Association, Suffolk; R & G Cuthbert, Herts; Guildhall Garden Products Ltd., Coventry; National Farmers' Union, London; Access, Northampton; Simplex of Cambridge Ltd; Banbury Buildings Ltd, Oxfordshire; George H. Elt Ltd, Worcester; Furnham Trading Ltd, Oxford; Bayliss Precision Components, Derbyshire; Samuel Dobie & Son Ltd, Clwyd; W.W. Johnson & Son Ltd, Lincolnshire; Dom Seeds, Lincolnshire; Warrick Propagators (Dependable Plastics Ltd), Essex; Landsmans Bookshop, Herefordshire; Kent Country Nurseries Ltd, Kent; Henry Doubleday Research Association, Essex; Mushroom Growers' Association, London; English Vineyards Association, Essex; T. Hulspas B.V., Maasdijk, Holland; Ken Muir, Essex; Nethergreen Products Ltd, Cheshire; Aerovap, Shepherd Aerosols Ltd, Kent; Humidifier Advisory Service, Kent; Osram-GEC, Middlesex; Greaves Air Systems Ltd, Chorley; Royal Botanic Gardens Kew, Surrey; Askham Bryan College of Argiculture and Horticulture, York; Gloucestershire College of Agriculture; East Malling Research Station, Kent; National Vegetable Research Station, Warwick; Glasshouse Crops Research Institute, Sussex; Agricultural Research Council, London; Leisure Services Committee Section, London Borough of Camden; Crittall Warmlife Ltd, Essex; B & V Parker (Chesterfield) Ltd, Hertfordshire; Pan Britannica Industries Ltd, Hertfordshire; Crescourt Loft Conversions, West Midlands; Gordon Hydroponics, Gloucestershire; Charley's Greenhouse Supplies, Washington DC; Indoor Light Gardening Society of America, Inc; Two Wests and Elliot Ltd, Derbyshire; Towlers Nurseries, Cambridge; Horticultural Education Association, Worcs; Tesco Group of Companies, Herts; The House of Rochford, Herts; Division of Agricultural Sciences, University of California.

Part One
THE ENVIRONMENT

Introduction

You need not live in the country, or even have a house with a garden, to enjoy your own home-grown and freshly-picked vegetables. Just consider the potential growing space that your urban dwelling does possess. Perhaps there is a balcony which could become home to anything from French beans to prize-winning marrows. If you are fortunate and live either at the top or bottom of a building, there may be access to a roof or patio. And many city windows will have outside window ledges, just waiting to sprout salad crops or a collection of herbs.

And there's no need to stop there. Indoor living spaces, usually neglected in the quest for green survival except for the odd aspidistra or Busy Lizzy, can also be fertile crop-growing areas. Inside window sills, or shelves built across them, will probably get enough light to grow exotics such as aubergine and peppers, not to mention an abundance of tomatoes. And even dingy places can be boosted with artificial growing lights. Your pantry will take on a new meaning if it is really used for growing food and not merely as a storage place. Some foods, such as sprouting seeds and mushrooms, will even thrive completely in the dark. There may be a spare room or unused loft space that could be entirely devoted to indoor farming, without any danger of leaks, rots, bugs and smells.

At any time of the year, 'while the winds whistle and the snows descend'*, you could be enjoying fresh food from your indoor farm, since you can control the 'climate'. After all, many orchid raisers are prepared to create special environments for their plants, so why not for fruit and vegetables, which

*William Cowper

11

can not only be eaten, but also enjoyed as beautiful house plants?

Despite today's interest in self-sufficiency, an indoor farm could obviously not come anywhere near to achieving complete self-sufficiency. But it would at least constitute an important first step towards cutting down dependence on the urban commercial nexus. The food you could grow will certainly gratify your taste buds, especially the summer treats that you can magic out of winter. And how many other relaxing and pleasurable activities could even lay claim to providing anything as near to our basic needs? The fruits of indoor farming can be a joy to look at and a delight to

consume, instilling a sense of pride as you sit down to a plate of home produce — if you can ever bring yourself to eat the end results of all that love and devotion.

It isn't hard to understand the recent revival in the enthusiasm for growing one's own fruit and vegetables. With the rising price of shop-bought foodstuffs, home-grown supplies make sense as far as any family budget is concerned. But it is more than a matter of plain economics. Freshly-picked produce is far tastier and, if cooked in the right way, much more nutritious than the alternatives in the supermarket that have spent a long time in transit, and on the shelf, before they eventually reach the shopping basket, en route to the cooking pot. In other words, you can *grow* better food than you can buy. You'll also enjoy types and varieties of vegetables that are rarely provided by the commercial growers who are governed in their choice by the dictates of mass marketing and mechanised farming techniques. Yield is more important to them than taste.

Vegetables produced at home are convenient, immediately to hand without shopping queues, parking difficulties or heavy loads to struggle with. It can take less time to grow them than to obtain them, and, apart from a few inexpensive items and packets of seed, their costs of production are largely a matter of your own time. And, as your own greengrocer, you will never have to worry about providing for surprise, and hungry, visitors.

But the sad fact of many people's town-tied lives is that they simply do not have the space to devote to vegetable plots. Most high-rise inhabitants in the cities don't even possess gardens, and municipal allotments have long waiting lists. Unlike in the United States, the idea of community gardening, on sites left temporarily vacant by city speculators, or perhaps other people's uncultivated gardens, is only in its infancy in Britain. And politically we are a long way off from the Chinese practice of growing food in such wasted areas as the strip of land by the side of the road.

Controlling the environment

If your first reaction to indoor farming is that it appears to be an 'unnatural' way to grow vegetables, consider the concept in relation to the way supposedly 'natural' gardening is carried out.

Few of the vegetables that we enjoy can grow in our climate without a great deal of human assistance. Watering or weeding outdoor crops or choosing particular varieties are the first steps along the road to artificial cultivation. Many vegetables have to be raised from seed indoors or within a greenhouse, as a protection against the elements, removing the activity further from the vagaries of nature and putting it under human control.

Horticulturists continually face the problem of attempting to raise varieties of vegetables in climates and at times of the year very different from their natural habitat. Only by controlling their overall development can individual vegetables be grown to finer quality and higher yields than they would if left to their own 'natural' devices.

The outdoor gardener or farmer is limited in his choices of what to grow by the seasons and the weather conditions of the area in which he lives. To a certain extent he can overcome these barriers by the use of greenhouses and the like. The indoor farmer, on the other hand, can exert a much fuller control over the environment in which the crops grow, and combine both natural and artificial factors to create the perfect conditions for growing more or less whatever he likes to eat.

While outdoor crops depend largely upon nature to provide their basic needs, indoors they will depend on you. If you fail them, your crops will grow at a feeble pace, awkwardly shaped, fail to flower or fruit, and probably die. The most crucial of these needs are: light, heat, water, food, air and humidity. They are interdependent but you must remember that no amount of increasing something a plant has enough of will compensate for something it lacks. You cannot turn up the thermostat on the central heating to make up for a shortage of light.

So we must look at these needs in turn to
understand what they mean to your future crops.

Light

The life of plants is basically devoted to the
business of building living tissue out of raw food
material. It is a process that is fundamental to every
form of life. The plants' food is derived from a
mixture of carbon dioxide, present in the air, and a
solution of mineral salts in the ground which are
absorbed through minute hairs on the roots. Unlike
animals and humans, fruits and vegetables cannot
live on solids.

The energy needed for combining and converting
water, minerals and carbon dioxide into food,
mainly carbohydrates, is obtained from light through
the chlorophyll pigment in the leaves. The process is
known as 'photosynthesis', and is determined both
by the intensity and duration of light falling on the
leaves. Photosynthesis, in turn, determines the rate
of growth of all fruits and vegetables (as well as
fruit setting and development).

The first likely obstacle that the indoor farmer
will come up against is insufficient light. Even plants
grown outdoors in the more northerly latitudes
suffer shortages of light during the short, cloudy
days of winter; the amount of light available from
November to January is only a fraction of that
during peak summer months. Without sufficient
light plants become etiolated, their stems becoming
elongated and leggy in appearance and the green
chlorophyll does not develop so that the plant looks
yellowy. Both their rate of growth and their shape
can be severely affected, as well as their fruiting
and flowering processes; low light levels can
adversely affect a plant's reproductive functions.

Fruits and vegetables grow best if they get plenty
of sunlight. As a very rough guideline, leafy
vegetables (lettuce, cabbage and so on) can stand
more shade than roots (beets, turnips, radishes)
which in turn can stand more shade than vegetable

fruit plants (tomatoes, courgettes, aubergines, cucumbers and peppers).

Crops cultivated on patios, balconies and roof areas are likely to get all the light they need, provided the area is not heavily shaded by other buildings or tall trees. South-facing areas are obviously in a better position to derive maximum benefit from the sun—in fact there may be a problem of their getting too much of a good thing—crops growing behind glass, for example, may need shading in mid-summer.

The amount of light received by plants growing in windows, both on inside sills and outside ledges, largely depends on the direction the window faces (as well as obstructions, curtains, overhangs and so on—an obstructed south-facing window may receive less light than an unobstructed north-facer). South-facing windows receive direct sunlight for a good part of the day, and when the weather is cloudy they will still be the areas receiving most of the light. They are usually the warmest places, irrespective of other forms of heating indoors, and all the fruiting vegetables will grow well in such a position. West windows are second best and should be light enough for tomatoes, as well as roots and leafy vegetables. East windows can be used for growing those vegetables that require the least amount of light. North windows will receive weak but constant light which will need to be supplemented by artificial lighting (see later).

The intensity of light on the inside of a window decreases according to the square of the distance from the window. In other words light falls off rapidly as you move back into the room, and you can easily see this for yourself by using an ordinary photographic light meter. The bigger the window, the wider its angle of 'view' and the further back you can go. Clearly, or rather unclearly, the more clouds, haze, city smog and dirt on the windows, the less the intensity of the light.

Any plant growing on the inside of a window receives only a half share of the available light coming from the outside. If you don't mind losing some of the room's light you can help compensate for this by using tin foil or mirror reflectors behind the plants. White walls will also help reflect what light there is. If your vegetables are growing in pots they can be turned occasionally to prevent their growing lopsidedly towards the light source, a process known as 'phototropism'. If it isn't practical to rotate the plant, either because the container cannot be turned, or if the amount of available light is too minimal for both sides to share, don't despair. The side of your vegetable that is away from the light will thin out, but this need not undermine the plant's overall well-being. You might also be able to follow the sun, moving plants during the day as the light changes, a luxury that the outdoor gardener does not have.

Temperature

Unlike fruit and vegetables grown outdoors, or even in a greenhouse, low temperatures are unlikely to be a limiting factor in indoor cultivation. As a general rule of thumb, the temperature that humans find comfortable to live in will also be satisfactory for home-grown food.

In the winter most homes tend to be heated to a daytime range between 65 and 72 degrees Fahrenheit, dropping to the low 60's at night. This will be perfect for most vegetables, especially the drop at night time which will coincide with their necessary dark rest period. If anything there is a danger indoors of the heat being too high for plants, especially if there is central heating. The idea that turning up the thermostat will increase the rate of growth of plants is a fallacy. High temperatures without accompanying high light intensity and humidity will result in poor growth. Even tropical house plants do not like very hot conditions because the amount of light and moisture in a room is much less than outdoors in the tropics, so their need for heat is correspondingly less. So, before you attempt to grow your first radish, invest in a thermometer, preferably a minimum-maximum type.

It is important to avoid fluctuating temperatures, for example by turning the central heating off in the middle of winter when everyone goes out to work during the day, or away for a weekend. Variations are only acceptable within a fairly narrow range.

Vegetables that need the most light generally require the highest temperature. Warm-season crops, those that are fruit bearing, such as tomatoes, peppers, aubergines, melons, courgettes and cucumbers, need long, warm days in order to ripen. They do best in a day temperature between 65 and 75 degrees fahrenheit, with a night-time temperature around 60 degrees. Cool-season crops, virtually all the roots (except sweet potatoes) peas, and most leafy vegetables, including the brassicas, are best grown between 55 and 65 degrees, with the important night-time temperature between 50 and 55 degrees. (Some plants are more governed by daytime temperature, others night.) Unless cool-season crops are kept cool their reproductive functions may be triggered off and they may produce seeds instead of luxuriant leaf and root development. Most of these crops are actually harvested in the middle of their life before they flower and set seed. A lettuce that 'bolts' for example, sending up its seed head, will not be good to eat.

If your home temperatures exceed the limits set by the particular vegetables you should definitely consider devoting one room to these plants and keeping it shut off from the rest of the house so that it can be kept cooler. By the same token, if your home is often left in a chilly state, keeping one room constantly at the required temperature will be more economical than having to maintain the right conditions throughout. Bear in mind that all crops will demand less warmth in the winter months when the light is poorer, unless supplemented by artificial light, since they will be 'resting' and so demanding less energy-making matter from the environment around them.

If your home is not centrally heated the type of heating most appreciated by vegetables would be a

18

greenhouse fan heater with a thermostat control and a fan to circulate the warmed air (and cool air during the summer months). This operates on the 'live air' principle, sucking in cold air at one end, heating it, and blowing it out at the other. The heated air rises through natural convection, circulates round the room, and then sinks to pass through the heater again. This movement of air is also beneficial to crops since still, cold and damp air can cause 'damping off' and other fungal diseases.

Greenhouse fan heaters have the added advantage of being designed for safe use in damp conditions. If you use other electrical installations you would be well advised to check with an electrician and change plugs, wiring and sockets to damp-proof materials since there will be a lot of water around and higher than usual levels of humidity.

While electricity may be the most expensive form of heating, it is certainly the most convenient and controllable, and perfect if you plan to automate your growing system (in conjunction with humidity, ventilation, lighting and so on). Unless there are strikes or power cuts, an automatically or thermostatically timed form of heating will allow you anxiety-free holidays away from the 'farm', mean less involvement in day-to-day repetitive operations, and a smaller risk of ruining a crop because of forgetting to do one vital thing at the right moment. Or remembering at the wrong time.

There are other forms of heating to consider. Tubular electric heaters are very popular in greenhouses since their heating element is completely sealed off. They are fairly inexpensive to run and would be well-suited for heating a room set aside for farming. Paraffin is even cheaper, and produces a heat high in humidity, but it cannot be automatically regulated and the heat it produces will not be evenly distributed. If you do use paraffin-heaters the wicks must be kept scrupulously clean and never allowed to smoke. No matter what form of heating you use, always stand your vegetables well away from the actual source of heat.

Double-glazed windows will help to conserve heat and cut the fuel bills. In addition to protection from the winter cold, the trapped layer of air between the glazed surfaces will help to cool the area immediately inside the window. Plants can stand almost touching the surface to gain maximum light without being burnt or frozen. Clear plastic can be used without any significant loss in daylight and would be the simplest material to install without paying for a builder to do it. Beware of cowboy double-glazing firms.

One final point that is sometimes overlooked in discussions about the heat requirements of plants: you must take precautions against the direct rays of the sun scorching plants that are growing behind glass. This is more a risk with greenhouses or cold frames (see chapter on growing under glass) but even sunny windows should have some form of shading (roller, slatted, or venetian blinds, or improvise with cheesecloth) to protect plants from intense heat. Some greenhouse roller shades are designed to allow light to pass while protecting plants from the more harmful effects of direct sunlight. Or you could brush on Coolglass electrostatic shading mixture and simply brush off later with a dry duster as conditions dictate.

Watering

It doesn't rain indoors (unless your roof leaks). Consequently all the water your crops need will have to be supplied by you.

Water is absorbed by the roots of the plant from the surrounding soil or potting compost. From there it is drawn up through the stem, along the branches or side shoots, and into the leaves. Water carries valuable nutrients from the soil to feed the plants and is needed to allow transpiration and photosynthesis to take place. Any water in excess of the plant's requirements evaporates, or is transpired, into the atmosphere through minute pores in the leaves.

Having said that, the greatest risk to all plants raised indoors is that they will be overwatered, killed by the misplaced kindness of their owner-growers.

Soil or compost that is completely saturated contains no air. Without a well-aerated soil, plant roots eventually rot. The root hairs are unable to absorb oxygen (or respire) and suffocate, and the plant itself droops, withers and finally dies. Excessive watering can also cause rot to the stem or fruit of a plant.

While all plants flourish best in a porous, well drained soil or compost, it is impossible to lay down hard and fast rules concerning the amount and frequency of watering. It will depend on many variables, including the size and the type of container, the time of year and the stage of growth of the plant, the amount of light, temperature and humidity, and, above all, on the type of fruit or vegetable.

Basically you should aim at keeping the compost moist, a balance between excess and denial. It's all right to let a plant get thirsty, but don't wait till it wilts before watering (plant cells are kept rigid by the presence of water; without it they collapse).

To test for moisture touch the surface of the compost or, better still, poke your finger about an inch below the surface. If it feels damp do not add water. You can also lay a piece of newspaper on the surface to see if it absorbs moisture. Even greater accuracy can be obtained with a moisture meter (like the one shown in the diagram). If the

compost needs water give it a proper drink, not a sprinkle, a mere promise.

Avoid watering to such a degree that it pours out of the pot's drainage holes, carrying away valuable nutrients. Pot saucers and drip trays were never designed to provide a puddle for the plant to stand in. The water should soak down, drawing air down to the roots. If the surface is too caked loosen it up, but gently, with a fork. Mind the roots.

And still more do's and don'ts. Take particular care not to overwater vegetables growing in decorative containers that do not have drainage holes through which surplus water can escape. The drainage material that you first put in the base of such containers will not actually get rid of water. It is there merely to hold water beneath the compost. It will only be absorbed by the compost when the latter dries out, and that will never happen if the compost is constantly saturated.

Water around the stems, not on them. This is particularly important with courgettes, cucumbers and melons. Water all vegetables in the morning and use tepid water—a cold shower can come as quite a shock to vegetables that have been sitting in a warm room. Use water from vegetable washings; cooking-water once it has cooled; and water draining from sprouting seeds: it will still retain some food value.

If you get water on the leaves, or if you have syringed them, don't put them straight into the sun as even miniscule droplets will act like the lens of a magnifying glass and, as every boy scout knows, that can cause painful scorching. An alternative method of watering smaller pots or seed trays is to half submerge them in a sink or bath and, when the air bubbles stop bubbling, remove and drain.

Humidity

Humidity refers to the amount of water vapour in the air. The chances are that the atmosphere in your home, with the possible exception of a frequently bathed-in bathroom, will be too dry for the successful cultivation of vegetables, especially if you have central heating.

The average outdoor level of relative humidity in Britain, for example, lies between 65% and 85%. In centrally heated homes this can drop to 25% or lower. The higher the temperature that you require to feel comfortable, the drier the air will be.

Temperature and humidity are interdependent. Humidity is a relative value; the warmer the air, the more water vapour it can hold before becoming saturated and condensing into actual droplets of water. A relative humidity of 80% at 68 degrees Fahrenheit for example, would fall to 44.5% at 77 degrees. Warm air will try to satisfy its thirst from wherever it can, by absorbing moisture from furniture, your skin, throat, and your growing vegetables. The loss from the latter is called transpiration. It often causes sore throats or headaches in people.

For the sake of your own well-being and that of your plants you should aim to live in a relative humidity of between 50% and 70%. At the very least you should scatter a few bowls of water around the room, although the evaporation from these will be rather insignificant in relation to the needs of the vegetables. An average size room, of 2500 cubic feet, with normal ventilation of two air changes an hour, maintained at 71 degrees with an existing relative humidity of 25% will require 1.4 pints of water every hour to maintain a level of 50%.*

More effective are the humidifiers that can be hung onto individual radiators. A daily mist spray with tepid water will help too, as well as keeping dust off the leaves. A much greater degree of humidity in the immediate vicinity of your crops can be created by standing the vegetables above a trayful of water, or placing the pots on a tray filled with sand, vermiculite, gravel or pebbles which are kept constantly wet. The evaporation of water from their surfaces will help keep the area round the plants high in humidity, but never let the plants actually stand in the water. The transpiration

*Humidity Advisory Service figures

process in the plants themselves will help raise the humidity level in their immediate vicinity. Stand all pots on a platform above their humidity beds — on oven grids, refrigerator racks or net fencing — or else there is a danger that the vegetables could become overwatered.

You can also create a humid micro-climate by standing individual plant-pots in an outer container and packing a moisture-retentive material such as peat or vermiculite between the two, and keeping it thoroughly and constantly moist. Humidity can be increased by generally splashing water around, a process known as 'damping down'. It is, of course, not always practical indoors.

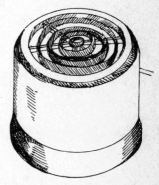

If you doubt whether the atmosphere is humid enough you should buy a hygrometer that will measure it for you. If the scale of your indoor farming is large, and the creation of micro-climates too limited a method, consider buying an electric humidifier, especially if you plan to devote an entire room solely to indoor farming. They can be automatically controlled to maintain a pre-set level of relative humidity by a device known as a humidistat (which does the same thing with humidity as a thermostat does with heat). Some electric humidifiers also remove dust, dirt and smoke particles, all arch enemies of growing crops. Some air conditioning units combine all these assets as well as keeping you cool.

The specific humidity requirements of particular vegetables varies. Tomatoes, for example, need a 'buoyant' atmosphere, whereas cucumbers prefer a steamy Turkish bath. But the basic guideline is to avoid a dry and stuffy atmosphere no matter what you choose to grow. In terms of beneficial side effects, humid air will reduce the plants' need for watering, keep the surrounding air cool in summer, and decrease the chances of red spider mite, an unwelcome pest. Too humid an atmosphere, however, can be harmful, causing fungal diseases, such as grey mould (Botrytis) or leaf mould on tomatoes.

Ventilation

Vegetables cultivated indoors grow best where currents of fresh air are freely circulating and changing around them.

A gentle breeze across the leaves of any plant causes water to evaporate (or transpire) through the leaf pores (known as stomata) and this, in turn, means that water will move up the plant from the roots, bringing nutrients from the surrounding soil or compost. If ventilation is poor the water vapour may condense on the leaf surfaces and cause disease. And while your vegetables will enjoy a reasonable level of relative humidity, ventilation will help prevent excesses here too which may lead to fungal diseases that thrive in stagnant, warm, moisture-laden air.

A well-ventilated room will also spread any heat around, so avoiding patches of excessive heat, and bring cooler air in from the outside. This will be particularly needed by plants standing in a sun-drenched window, or completely under glass, where the heat build-up in summer may be far too great for their comfort.

In commercial nurseries the air is often artificially enriched with carbon dioxide. Humans will probably produce sufficient for any amount of crops grown indoors especially if you talk to them, but effective ventilation will help replenish the carbon dioxide round the leaves that has been absorbed by the plant during the process of photosynthesis. As long as there is light, all plants take in carbon dioxide and give off oxygen. At night photosynthesis ceases and plants absorb oxygen from the atmosphere and emit carbon dioxide.

Although ventilation is vital it does not imply that plants are fresh air freaks. Good ventilation does not mean draughts, especially chilling ones from the outside winter air. These can kill a crop, so open windows only during the warmer months for a gentle movement of fresh air. In the winter keep out the cold, damp, foggy and frosty atmosphere, and take the added trouble of taping over any gaps in ill-fitting window frames or doors with masking tape or draught-excluder strips. Open windows in an adjacent room so that the outside air has a chance to warm up a bit before meeting the vegetables. Insulation will help save on your fuel bills too, and will help granny's rheumatism.

The simplest way to guarantee a constant and gentle re-circulation of the air, apart from opening windows, is with a small electric fan. If you use a greenhouse type electric fan heater to provide warmth during the winter it can be used during the summer with just the fan. Otherwise buy a small electric fan, but never aim it directly at anything growing as the air current could prove tantamout to a lethal draught.

If you have some outside room for a small patio greenhouse, or are prepared to devote a spare room entirely to raising vegetables, an automatic vent would be ideal, since it will be ruled by the prevailing temperature, operating quickly and without any help from you in response to changing conditions. While you are out working in your town factory or office, or off for a weekend, you won't have to worry about a sudden change in the weather spoiling your crops. If you install an extractor fan to remove the stagnant air, and an intake unit to bring in the fresh, place the former as high as you can so that it takes away the rising hot air, and the latter at a low level. Or buy a single unit that combines both functions. Again, instead of an electric system you may be able to fit a thermo-expansion opener.

A note about air pollution

Stuffy and stagnant air will be harmful to any plant grown indoors, especially where the air is laden with pollutants such as cigarette smoke, dust, paint, gas fumes, coke and anthracite fires and unclean oil heaters. (Natural gas, in fact, will not harm vegetables; in fact its carbon dioxide enrichment of the air will be welcomed.) Hold a party in your farm room and the crops could suffer a mighty setback to their growth, far more severe than your own hangover. If you must celebrate in your city jungle make sure the room is well ventilated.

Plants growing in an urban environment are said to receive 16 per cent less light than they did a generation ago.

The soot, smoke and fumes of the city air, by coming in between the chlorophyll pigments on the leaves and the sunlight, lower plants' ability to photosynthesise. They block the leaf pores so that the vegetables have difficulty in breathing, or transpiring. And if you live in a heavily industrialised city where the air is a permanent filthy haze, the toxic impurities won't exactly enhance the flavour and freshness of your vegetables. They will not help your healthy growth either.

Remove as much pollution from the vegetables as you can, firstly by dusting with a dry cloth, then syringing with a fine mist spray or wiping down foliage where possible with clean tepid water, a mixture of water and milk or a mild soap solution (not detergent) and a piece of cheese cloth or sponge. Don't touch the leaves of seedlings as they are too delicate to be cleaned. Beyond that there is little that can be done. No one really knows the full effects of metal poisons from cars, or factory impurities, on vegetables.

Compost and fertilisers

When growing vegetables in containers never use garden soil. It becomes too tightly packed together and will be a likely carrier of diseases and pests. The money you save by importing it from the countryside, a neighbour's garden, or a nearby park under the cover of night, will not be worth it.

Always use compost, sowing-compost for seeds and potting-compost when you transplant the seedlings to their second and subsequent containers. Buy a standardised mixture from a reliable shop, but remember that these do not represent proprietary brands. Your only guarantee that the compost is good will depend on the reputability of the place it comes from.

Basic compost is a mixture of sand, peat and loam. Their relative proportions are often marked on the bag, so 1-1-1 for example means they are equally mixed. There are also soil-less composts available that are made up of a mixture of peat and vermiculite plus fertilisers. Again, you could mix up your own compost, equally divided between peat, potting-soil and vermiculite (or sand, in which case get coarse builder's sand, and never use seaside sand as the salt can never be washed out entirely and its residue can kill your vegetables).

Composts are clean, odourless and usually lighter to move around than soil. Their sterility guarantees their freedom from pests, weeds and diseases, and they have an ideal texture both for drainage and the movement of air around the roots of the plants growing in them. Composts also contain all the essential plant foods, including the important nitrogen, phosphorus and potassium plus other essential minerals, and these will be sufficient to sustain growth for quite a while before they need boosting. Keep the compost well aerated by 'digging' it every so often with a fork, but mind you don't damage any tender roots. Just break up the surface gently every two or three weeks. Change your compost for new supplies every two or three years by which time it will have become sour, lost its texture, and may well be tainted by city pollution.

While composts do have their own built-in plant nutrients, these will become exhausted before the plants reach maturity. You will have to make up these deficiencies. One of the key differences between vegetables grown in pots, tubs or boxes and those grown in a garden or allotment is that the compost represents the vegetable's only possible source of water and food. We have already dealt with water. The roots of the plant cannot stretch out into the surrounding soil for fresh sources of nourishment once they have used up those in the container. You must feed them, and so replace the used-up nutrients, either by a combination of intuition and the instructions on the labels and in the section on individual vegetables, or by purchasing an electronic soil analyser to gauge both the moisture and fertiliser content of the compost.

Liquid fertiliser is the easiest to use with containerised vegetables. It comes in both organic (liquid manure or seaweed preparations) and inorganic (chemical) forms, so make your choice according to what you ultimately want to do to your body. Compound fertilisers, organic or inorganic, contain a balanced mixture of nitrogen (that promotes general and leaf growth), phosphorous (that encourages root formation, as well as flowering and seeding) and potassium (for flower development and the general health of the plant). N, P and K are used as their respective abbreviations. The proportions between each is expressed numerically, in other words a 9-7-6 fertiliser represents 9% nitrogen availability, 7% phosphorous and 6%

potassium. The balance you need will depend on what's growing; tomatoes, for example, require a fertiliser higher in potassium, but you won't go wrong by playing it safe with a general compound fertiliser that has a similar amount of all three. It will also include calcium, magnesium, sulphur and iron in lesser amounts, and minute quantities of many other 'trace' elements (boron, manganese, molybdenum, zinc, copper and chlorine). If you're a very particular sort of person you could always test your soil and rectify particular deficiencies until the balance is just right in which case you should buy the ingredients separately and mix up your own.

Always follow the manufacturer's instructions with regard to the dilution and frequency of fertilising your crops. As with watering, plants are often over-fed, especially by busy city folk, which can cause root damage, and unnecessary bank balance damage. Plants can only absorb a certain amount of fertiliser at any one time, so never over do it. Always apply when the compost is moist and use a fine rose-head watering can. Don't let the fertiliser fall on the leaves unless you are using 'foliar feed' which is sprayed onto both sides of the foliage and from there it is absorbed directly into the plant. Spray according to the directions and never on plants standing in the sun as their leaves will scorch.

You could also recycle some of your kitchen waste, such as peelings, vegetable scraps, leftovers, eggshells, coffee grounds and so on by mixing them with plenty of water. Use vegetable cooking water, and blend everything together in an electric blender. Use this 'organic soup' on your crops every couple of weeks. It is not a true organic compost (as distinct from seed or potting compost) since it does not contain bacteria, but it does return lots of valuable nutrients to your growing vegetables.

You can make organic compost out of natural waste material if you have a small outdoor area — a balcony, patio or backyard — using a plastic bag or rubbish bin that can be sealed to keep animals out and smells in. The simplest way is to make a few drainage holes in a polythene bag and build up alternate layers of vegetable waste, soil or peat, and a proprietary compost activator to help the rotting process in place of manure. When the bag is full tie it up and stick it out of the way till you need it. The bigger your composting scale, the higher the temperature that can be retained, and the quicker the ingredients will break down.

The Environmental Education Committee of Rochester, New York suggests using two galvanised dustbins, with well-fitting lids and holes drilled round the bottom, standing off the ground on bricks. The base of each bin is filled with a 3 inch layer of soil, on top of which vegetable waste matter is added and a layer of soil, grass clippings, dried manure or shredded newspaper every few inches. The Committee recommends putting angleworms or earthworms (red worms) in the can to help break down the contents. Every two weeks the contents of the first bin is tipped into the second and back again two weeks later, keeping the muck moist but not soaking. It should be ready for use after two or three months, when the individual ingredients are no longer discernible. Mix it up with your potting compost. Such a composting unit can be kept in the cellar, although you'll need something underneath the cans to catch the drips (which won't smell and can be used on your vegetables).

31

Pollination

With the exception of frame cucumbers you must pollinate your fruit-bearing vegetables (tomatoes, beans, aubergines, courgettes and peppers) by hand so as to encourage the formation of fruit. The natural means of pollination, by insects, water or the wind for example, will not occur inside an enclosed area. So use a camel-hair brush, or a feather, to brush the pollen from the anther of one flower to the stamen of another. The female flowers

male

female

of courgettes, the ones with the tiny fruit appearing behind, should be fertilised with a male flower by removing the latter flower, folding back the petals and holding it over the female so that they touch. Tomatoes are best pollinated by tapping the stems daily once the flowers appear, and spraying with a fine mist of water. If your crops still fail to fruit after such careful pollination, the reason could be insufficient light, lack of water (or irregular watering) or failure to pinch out trailing varieties.

Containers

The two golden rules for choosing your containers are that they must be deep enough to provide an adequate depth of compost for the particular fruit or vegetable that they are to house, and that they must be provided with good drainage facilities. Beyond that the range of possibilities is as limited as your imagination.

Nearly all of the 'conventional' pots and containers will have built-in drainage holes. The Great Pot Controversy, whether clay or plastic pots are better for your vegetables, is all rather a horticultural red herring. A lettuce grown in one won't taste any different from one raised in the other. But it is true that clay pots are porous, allowing both water and air to pass through the sides, so that the roots can breathe a little more easily, although the compost will tend to dry out more quickly as a consequence and therefore needs more watering. Clay pots are also heavier but lovelier to look at than plastic, except, that is, when algae form on the outside, a harmless but ugly disadvantage. Plastic pots are cheaper to buy. Both sorts can be stood in drip catching saucers, placed on shelves, plant stands, hung in macramé and other fancy holders, or mounted on walls with special hooks.

Hanging baskets come in all forms, from the purely functional to the highly decorative. Some are sold with macramé rope or leather holders, and there are also hanging devices made from perspex and nylon fishing-line so that they are almost invisible. They are quite readily obtained from garden shops.

Window boxes (see the section on window-box growing) are chiefly made from plastic, polystyrene, fibre glass and wood. Many can be used both on outside and inside window sills. They are deep enough to take the roots of most vegetables.

Strawberry urns or pots can grow other things besides strawberries, herbs being perhaps the most appealing to look at. The clay ones are much more expensive to buy than the plastic 'tower' pots.

Decorative pots, either sold specifically as plant holders, or adapted for that use from your own favourite ceramics, must have provision made for drainage — for which see later.

Grow-bags have revolutionised both the commercial production of certain vegetables as well as the home-grown, and for the town dweller they are of special merit since they neither have nor need drainage holes and so can be stood anywhere, even in the middle of an antique Persian carpet, as long as they get sufficient light.

The bags are made out of polythene and filled with sterilised peat, fertilisers (enough to sustain growth for a few weeks without supplementary liquid feeding) and lime to counteract the peat's acidity. They are most advantageously employed for growing the big exotics — tomatoes, aubergines, courgettes and peppers — in restricted areas. You can get three or four plants to a bag and they will run far less risk of disease than those grown by any other method. They can also be used for almost any other vegetable, such as lettuce, beans, onions, strawberries, cauliflowers and so on. While the manufacturers don't recommend their use for a second growing season, you could boost it for another crop with fertilisers and stand a pretty good chance of success. Use one left vacant by tomatoes for a succession crop of lettuces.

Grow-bags are not hard to make and could save you quite a bit of money if you want more than one or two. Use non-transparent, heavy-duty polythene. Cut a piece 50 inches by 30 inches and staple it (using the heavy duty kind, and lots of them) together along the long side and close up one end. Keep the long seam in the middle and on the underside. Line the bottom with another piece of polythene, glued over the seam and fill with compost. You can buy grow-bag kit ingredients from chemical firms — look for their advertisements in the gardening magazines — and mix with peat. Fill and staple the other end together. Cut three or four 8-inch crosses, fold the flaps under and plant.

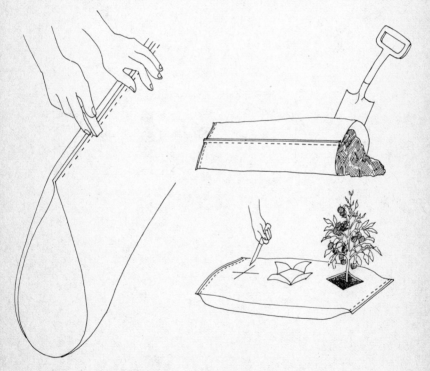

Lots of household throwaways can be recycled to make excellent containers for growing vegetables.

Tins: coffee, caterer's or restaurant's giant tins; oil cans.
Ceramic fittings: sinks, baths, bidets, chamber pots, cattle troughs.

Building supplies: chimney pots, drain pipes, guttering, bricks and roofing felt..

Baskets: Laundry, picnic hampers, clothes baskets, waste paper baskets, supermarket trolleys — can all be lined with heavy duty polythene.

Kitchen equipment (again, caterer's size if you can):
pots, pans, buckets, vegetable racks, fridge
crispers, bread bins.

Children's outgrowns: paddling pools, trolleys,
prams.

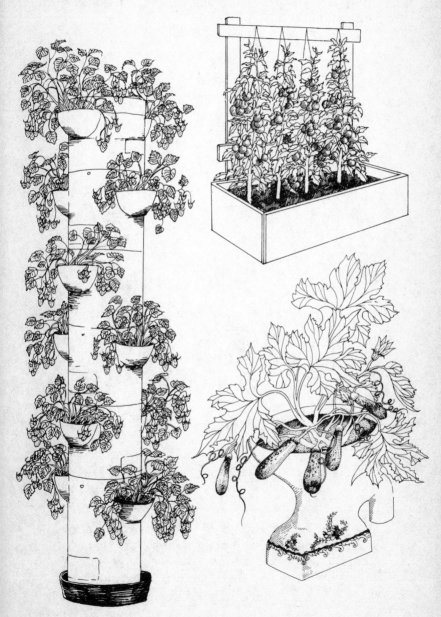

Other things: garden pools; wire or glass lampshades for hanging baskets; car tyre (cut in half); motor battery cases; tea chests; aquaria; ammunition boxes; galvanised and plastic water tanks; cut down plastic containers; fruit boxes; expanded polystyrene packing round TV's, etc. Or anything else you can think of.

For propagation you could use some of the above, as well as yogurt pots, margarine tubs, plastic cups or bags, milk cartons and cut down detergent-bottles, photographic trays, cat-litter trays and so on.

If your containers look unsightly cover them with tin foil or paint. Mount big ones on castors so that you can take advantage of the passing sunshine and allow plants to be turned to allow for symmetrical growth. Wheel indoors for artificial light set-ups, or just to have around as a talking point.

Wooden containers should be painted on the inside with bituminous paint (with a petrol base, never coal tar as this will be harmful to the plants) or line with heavy duty polythene. Glass containers should be painted on the outside to keep the light off the roots.

Good drainage is essential for all containers. (Wet feet can be fatal as plants will suffer from an oxygen shortage at their roots.) There are three possibilities. Containers that already have drainage holes, such as flower pots, need only to be crocked in the usual way, by placing bits of broken pots and other ceramic breakages over the holes, or cover the bases of large containers, such as window boxes, with nylon gauze. Drainage can be further helped by covering the bottom with an inch layer of gravel or small stones. You can use saucers, aluminium pie-dishes or trays to collect seepage and prevent it spilling on the floor. If the drainage holes lie underneath the containers stand the containers on jam jar lids or cotton bobbins to raise above the ground.

If the container does not have drainage holes but would not split, crack or shatter if you drilled some, or punched them out with a hammer and nail, do so. Holes are often best made along the sides as bottom drilling may weaken the container's structure and compost-holding strength. Crock and cover with an inch of gravel (or you could crock, add an inch layer of vermiculite, an inch of peat and then compost). Excess water will then be held by the peat and vermiculite instead of dripping out and will replenish the compost as it dries out.

If you use solid containers in which it is impossible to drill or punch holes, they should be deep enough to allow at least a 2-inch layer of gravel, preferably with some charcoal mixed in, before adding compost. Always take particular care not to overwater such containers. Similarly, since they do not have provision for drainage, grow-bags must never be allowed to become waterlogged, or to dry out as the peat may lose its absorbent properties.

It is hard to tell just how big a fruit or vegetable will grow by the time it reaches full maturity, although the variety's description in the seed catalogues and on the seed packets will give you a fairly good idea. While vegetable yields will suffer if you cram them too close together, you can economise on the spacings recommended on the seed packets if you plan on harvesting while the vegetables are still young and tender. Many vegetables can have their top growth pinched back if they grow too tall and you want to encourage their bushy development, but their growth underground is more relevant to your container decision. You can grow deep rooters only in deep pots. If a plant should become pot-bound you will have to move it to a larger container, so if you are using decorative and awkwardly-shaped containers which will never allow the plant to simply slip out, be sure they are big enough to cope in the first place. Otherwise it will have to be a choice between pot or plant.

Window boxes

Add up the total length of the window-sill area in your apartment or flat or house. You will undoubtedly be surprised by the amount of farming space that you have been neglecting. Even if your casement windows open outwards you can still hang window boxes below the window, safely fastened with brackets, and they will have the added bonus of not depriving the room of any light. Make sure they are low enough so that the opening window clears the growing crop. Which ever way you use them, window box farming will not only provide you with a plentiful supply of fresh food, but also add a little colour to drab urban streets.

Gardening stores stock a wide range of ready-to-use window boxes, made in varying lengths and out of different materials, such as plastic, polystyrene and fibreglass. They also make excellent general purpose vegetable containers for use in other parts of the house, particularly along the inside length of a window.

But why not make your own, tailored to the exact size of the sills, so that you can cram the most into the sill area? For super crammers, consider extending the actual length and width of the sill by securely fixing a plank that is a bit longer and wider than the sill it stands on.

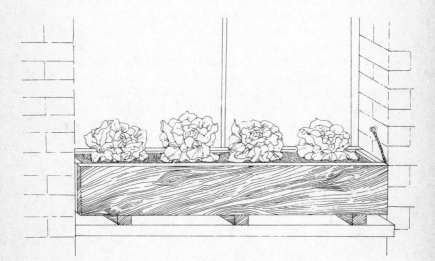

To make a box use 1 inch thick timber (the harder the better), 9 inches wide (the ideal depth for a box). Work out the precise dimensions of each box, saw the wood accordingly, and assemble using nails or, for a more professional job, brass screws and corner brackets. Craftsmen will be able to dovetail the lengths together. Make the box a little shorter than the sill length if you want to be able to move it in and out of the room without help or hernia. A handle screwed onto each end will help you to manoeuvre it.

Drill several ½ inch drainage holes along the bottom of the box, or burn them out with a red-hot poker as charred wood is more water resistant. Fix two or three sloping wooden wedges on the bottom to allow air to pass underneath and water to drain away. If your boxes are likely to drip on the heads of people below or stain your outside walls, you should place drip trays underneath the boxes to catch the seepage. If you crock and add vermiculite and peat below the compost, there will be minimal drip.

Paint the inside of the box with a non-creosote wood-preservative to protect the wood against wet rot and then with a coat of bituminous paint. You can also make the wood water resistant by painting the inside with paraffin and setting light to it. Hardly a wise move if you live in a flat, but if you can find space to do it outside let the flames burn for a minute of two and then turn the box upside down to extinguish.

Fix the boxes securely to the walls of your building using metal brackets, hook and eye screws or retaining chains. The most innocent crop of pixie tomatoes could make a dangerous impact on life below if they were to be blown off by a gust of wind, or knocked off by a playful pet.

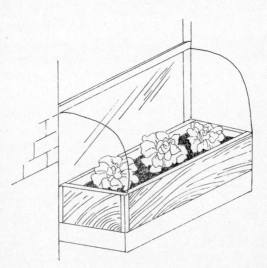

Before filling the boxes with compost, to within an inch of the top, crock in the usual way. Instead of filling with compost you could use the boxes to house a row of pots.

Consult the section on individual vegetables before deciding what to grow. Salad crops are an obvious choice, including lettuce, spring onions and radishes, but any of the shallower rooting varieties of vegetables will be fine. Herbs are a good choice too, especially handy on a kitchen sill.

If you are growing crops from seed you would be advised to propagate some of them indoors, wherever suitable, both to give them a warm and early start to life, and leave your boxes free for other vegetables until the seedlings are sturdy enough to be transplanted to the outside. To protect seedlings and delicate crops from the sometimes harsh conditions outdoors you can 'greenhouse' windowsills by covering with a screen of corrugated transparent plastic, sealed off at the ends, or use ordinary gardener's cloches. Alternatively, make a lean-to tent arrangement, held away from the plants by galvanised wire hoops (made from coathangers) that enclose the box and the window as a whole growing compartment. The area can be warmed by leaving the window open so that room air can enter,

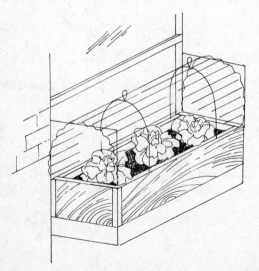

and kept ventilated in the summer in the same way. Smaller seedlings can be protected by jam jars or plastic bags provided they do not come into contact with the leaves. Apart from weather protection, such coverings will also help to keep city fumes and smutty bits off your future dinner, and greedy birds from getting it before you do. Nets will also keep away cheeky sparrows and other scavengers.

Outdoor areas

If your home has any sort of outdoor area, such as a balcony, terrace or access to a flat roof, it will probably offer considerable growing potential. A word of warning, however, before you start loading it up with containers and compost by the sackful: if

there is any doubt as to whether the structure can bear all the additional weight that your farming plans entail, be sure to check with an architect or official surveyor who will advise you on whether the wooden beams or concrete lintels will stand the burden. It is most important to check up in the case of back roof extensions where supporting beams may be designed only to hold up the ceiling and roof lining. If that's the case you will have to strengthen the joists or just limit the roof farm to a few pots, smaller containers, or grow-bags. Also, if the prevailing winds are strong, protect the growing area with side screens which, in turn, will protect you from toppling off the edge.

Most balconies are built to carry quite a substantial weight, especially in reinforced concrete buildings, so your urban farm is unlikely to endanger the structure. Start off by painting any surrounding walls white so that the light will be reflected to where it is needed most. The walls, and any side trellis work that may have to be erected to shelter plants from the wind (the higher you are the windier it will be) can be employed to support climbing varieties of vegetables, such as peas, beans and

cucumbers. Train them to creep up railings and ugly drainpipes too. In fact, wherever space is limited, think vertically and you'll probably double it.

See if you can fit, and afford, a mini-greenhouse. The gardening market has recently been flooded with such models, designed with the small-space grower in mind. At least try to make some sort of glassed-in, and heated, area. It would extend the growing season, enabling you to overwinter some leafy crops, bring forward the outdoor season of others, and it would be a summer home to weather-sensitive melons or peppers. But more about that in the next chapter.

Apart from an attractive range of larger containers, shop-bought or improvised, you will get the best return from a balcony by constructing terraces out of 9 inch deep boxes (or use ordinary window boxes), arranged as the illustration shows, facing the sunniest direction. 'Gutter' them so that excess water can soak away where you want it to, and not dribble back over the living room carpet. These troughs can also hang outside the balcony as long as you fasten them securely. Follow the rules for window box gardening.

Try vegetable 'tree' gardening. Make a frame out of 2 by 1 inch rot resistant wood, and nail standard chicken wire across all sides. Line the insides with plastic (or use sphagnum moss) and fill the inside area with potting compost. Poke holes in the plastic and plant in the sides and along the top. Another type of 'tree' can be made from a pole, stood on a stable cross base, with pots fastened onto the pole by metal pot holders.

Growing behind glass

Every home has a window, usually several, and they should be the first place that an indoor farmer looks to when assessing his growing space. They not only guarantee a source of natural light, the strength of which will depend on the direction the window faces, but the glass itself will help to both trap and retain heat generated by the sun.

Growing on the inside can mean more than shoving a table in front of the window and standing one or two pots there. In the first place there is no reason to restrict its scope to just a one-level spread. Build two or three shelves across the window, mounted on shelf brackets attached to the sides of the window frame, and use them to support rows of pots. The shelves can be made from wood or glass which will allow more light to reach the plants, but for safety's sake use toughened plate glass with rounded edges. If your home has small children or frisky pets use wood and make holes into which the pots can be fitted. Line the holes with polythene to prevent water dripping on the floor. Oven grids could be tied together with rope one above the other as an alternative form of tiered shelving. And any woodworker who knows his onions could construct a shelf unit combined with a desk base. Instead of trying to draw inspiration for letters from a landscape of urban ugliness you could brood upon a pot or two of rosemary and thyme.

Suspended from the top of the window and mounted on a bracket, or from hooks in the ceiling joists, could be hanging baskets, with strawberries trailing down the sides perhaps. Hang them high enough so that you won't clump your head, but low enough to reach with a watering can. They dry out faster than ordinary pots. Line with sphagnum moss (or polythene—green looks nice) and attach by swivel hooks so that they can be turned to spread the sunlight all round.

Most other containers will work well in conjunction with window space, from plastic window boxes used on the inside to grow-bags. Climbing vegetables, say runner beans with scarlet flowers, could be trained up lengths of bamboo secured to the sides of the box, and make perfect curtains by the time they reach the top of the window. All such growths will, of course, be at the expense of the room's daylight. You'll have to decide which rates higher in terms of your living environment.

Bay windows are excellent for indoor vegetable

cultivation, since the area will receive light from three sides. You could construct a sand-filled staging tray that fits the entire bay and connect it to an automatic watering device, with artificial lighting as well so that the switched-on sunshine will boost your vegetables' growth as well as show off the area in the evenings.

Don't overlook a skylight window. If the light is bright enough you may be able to induce a climber to reach for the sky. Otherwise hanging baskets are probably the most suitable containers to use.

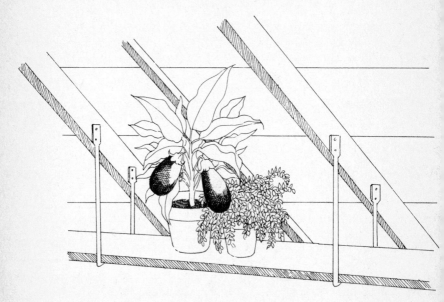

The previous chapter described various ways in which outside window boxes can be 'cloched' to derive maximum benefit from the sun. Miniature window greenhouse units are a relatively recent addition to the ever-increasing range of horticultural products on the market. There could be no finer investment for the indoor farmer. By turning an ordinary window into a bay they actually enlarge the size of indoor space, and many more blocks of flats will probably be covered with them a few years hence. They provide ideal conditions for growing either an impressive range of house plants or, more to the point, vegetables.

You may, however, need official permission from
someone or other before erecting a window
greenhouse, so find out before you buy or build.
Since their structure is sound and they can be
securely attached to any building, it is unlikely that
any objection would be reasonable.

Their size can range from the small 'nature
bubbles' which are really no more than a 'glass-
housed' window box, to larger units that extend
outwards to a distance of 2 feet. They can either be
fixed to your building to cover an existing window, a
sort of reach-in affair with access from indoors
through the window itself, or they can be hung onto
a wall for use on a balcony or patio. They can also
be rigged up with artificial lights to supplement

winter sunshine and provide an interesting night-time alternative to those brocade curtains.

The types that cover an existing window will not require their own source of heating as the warm house air will do the job through the window opening. This will also provide a measure of ventilation too, but in the summer the models that have additional ventilators are a better buy. Keep the window closed and you could seal off the unit from the house and create an entirely independent growing chamber, with its own heating, ventilation and humidity operating independently from the home environment. You could create a similar environment by blocking off a bay window from the rest of the room with transparent fibreglass or plastic. In such a window conservatory the conditions of, say, a tropical rain forest could be established, although such an atmosphere would be more practical for the cultivation of exotic house plants than vegetables.

In Victorian times the larger conservatories were
built to function very much as part of the home
living area, quite unlike the remote greenhouse
structures that can often be found lurking
somewhere near the bottom of the suburban garden.

For city growers there are several mini greenhouse
models available that will fit into the tiniest of
backyards, in narrow passages between houses, on
roof areas or patios, and on balconies. If you get
bitten by the growing bug it would be worth
considering one, especially as they can become
conservatory-like in their physical attachment to

your home. On a balcony, for example, a small greenhouse with a sliding door could be aligned to fit over the room's access door.

Unless the planned location is an extremely
awkward shape the pre-fabricated kit structures are
the most economical to buy. Send away for several
manufacturers' catalogues before committing
yourself, and see which model would best suit your
home and your pocket. Some smaller models can,
in fact, be turned into a variety of shapes both to
accommodate either vertical crops like tomatoes, or
horizontals such as melons, or to fit into a limited
area.

Storm porches, or any sort of enclosed glass
verandah, will offer similar protection, but since the
frequent opening and closing of the outer door will
allow chilling draughts to enter, grow only hardy
vegetables if the porch is your main gateway to the
outside world.

Any area covered or enclosed by glass, or shatter-
proof plastic, fibreglass or plastic sheeting, will
lengthen the growing season, and thereby effectively
extend your farming resources. Your crops will ripen
before they ever appear in the shops, and still be
cropping later in the year when their shop-sold

brothers are costing an exorbitant amount. The material you use will not only trap the sun's light and heat, but also protect plants from wind and frost, and city pollution.

If you create the right conditions in the mini-greenhouse, regarding heat, ventilation, humidity and light, supplementing natural 'supplies' wherever necessary, the choice of vegetables that can be grown is virtually unlimited, and their yields will be magnificent. An experiement in the United States, for example, conducted on behalf of the Vegetable Factory, is reported to have produced 650 pounds of vegetables in a year using a greenhouse area only 8 feet by 12 feet.

On the smallest scale you should at least consider making cold frames (from old casement windows on top of a wooden frame) or buying a few for a balcony or terrace area. Use them to house either potted vegetables, except those that grow too tall, or fill with compost for direct planting. Line the base with a bed of sand or gravel to assist drainage.

If you insulate and equip a cold frame with soil-, and perhaps air-warming cables it becomes a warm frame, so to speak, and perfect for growing melons,

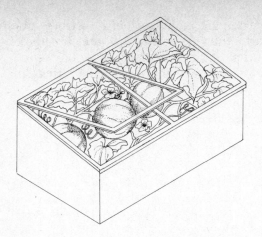

courgettes and cucumbers, as well as raising winter
salads. Open all frames during warm days to
ventilate and prevent overheating, but close at
night. In the winter, if frost seems likely, cover with
a blanket. In the summer whitewash the glass to
prevent the sun scorching the plants.

Whatever type of structure you decide upon, its
orientation will be important. Position it to face in
as southerly direction as can be managed. The
actual angle of the slope will affect the amount of
light that will penetrate, the optimum being when
the angle of incidence of the sun is as near 90
degrees as possible (actual insolation will depend on
latitude and the time of the year). The slope will
also permit rain water to run off. Don't overlook the
need to shade your crops from the rays of a direct
summer sun. And remember that the whole object
of the exercise will be lost if you fail to keep the
surfaces clean. City muck will cut out the valuable
light.

Farming under artificial light

One of the most recent and revolutionary
developments in horticulture has been the increasing
use of artificial light, both commercially, especially
for vegetable propagation, and domestically for the
cultivation of the more exotic house plants. For

indoor farmers it is the perfect answer for poorly-lit city apartments, especially in winter time when artificial lighting can be used to supplement inadequate natural light, or for converting dim corners into salad farms.

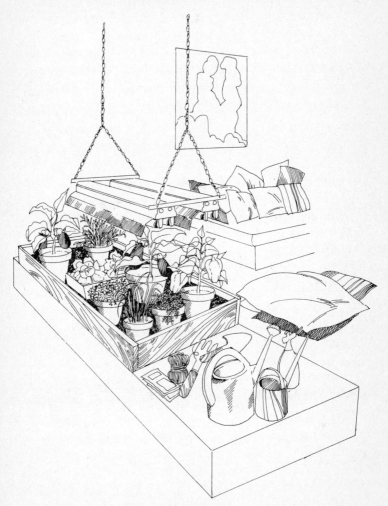

While it is true that plants are not fussy whether the light they require comes from the sun or not, it is important that the wavelengths of the light they absorb are correctly balanced for photosynthesis. The growth of all plants is affected in a very complex way by the actual spectrum of light, and the more that artificial lighting is used as the sole source of light, the more important it becomes to get the balance right. Visible light is made up of a number of different colours, as any rainbow will tell you. The colour of the light we see depends on its wavelengths. This quality of light is not something we normally observe with the eye, nor can it be measured with a photographic light meter as can its overall intensity.

Consequently, before designing any sort of artificial light set-up, there are three broad areas to consider: the light intensity (in other words how strong it is), the light duration (the amount of time the light is actually on), and the colour or wavelength balance.

LIGHT INTENSITY

Vegetables need a far greater intensity of light when grown indoors than ordinary room light. Even on a dull day, the light outdoors will be much brighter than we may realise. Plants grown in the open can receive as much as 10,000 foot candles from the sun at noon in the peak of summer, to a winter low of around 900. The term foot candle is a measure of light intensity: what the plant actually receives. (One foot candle of light is the amount produced in a dark room by a special candle on a surface that is one foot away from the flame. Two foot candles is the amount of light produced by two foot candles, and so on. Light can also be measured in lumens, which refer to the output of the lamp, or visible light. The metric equivalent is lux or kilolux.) Foot candles can be measured by a special foot candle meter, or you can convert ordinary photographic light-meter readings by the following formula:

$$B = \frac{20(f)^2}{TS}$$

Where B is the illumination in foot candles
  f is the aperture, the f stop on the camera or meter
  T is the shutter speed in seconds
  S is the ASA rated film speed.

A light level of about 1000 foot candles, for example, would be the equivalent of an ASA rating of 75, f8 aperture and an exposure of about 1/60th of a second.

Approximate foot-candle values on plants using two 40-watt fluorescent lamps

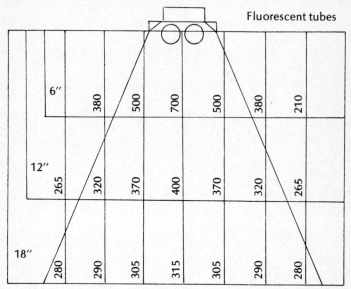

Fluorescent tubes

6"	380	500	700	500	380	210
12"	265	320	370	400	370	320	265
18"	280	290	305	315	305	290	280

The intensity of your lighting set-up will depend on the number of lamps used, their power, and the distance they are from the growing area. A basic 4 foot by 1 foot arrangement, using two 4 foot, 40 watt fluorescent tubes positioned roughly 4 inches apart and 3 or 4 inches above the plants, mounted in a reflector so that the precious light is not dissipated into non-growing areas, would produce 20 watts per square foot of growing area and about 1000 foot candles, sufficient for most vegetables. If you use more tubes the size of the growing area would be larger (four 4 foot tubes would light an area 3 foot by 4 foot to sufficient intensity for vegetable growth). Longer tubes will be more efficient if you have the room; an 8 foot tube emits more light than two 4 foot tubes.

Roots and leafy vegetables would flourish with 1000 foot candles operating for 14 to 16 hours a day, the approximate equivalent to the amount of daylight they would need for optimum growth. Since the fruiting vegetables require much more light, up to 2500 foot candles, they cannot be grown solely under artificial light and would have to be grown under a combination of daylight and artificial light. You could use the High Intensity Discharge lamps that the commercial growers employ, but only the keenest amateur growing on a big scale would be justified in doing so since their capital and running costs are high. HIDs also require specialised equipment and knowledge before they can be successfully used.

The smaller types of vegetable will obviously do best under artificial lights because the whole plant would then receive maximum intensity from the lamps. Herbs and salad crops are the ones that are best suited to such cultivation methods, but experiment with any of the small varieties. If you design a vertical lighting arrangement you could also raise taller vegetables. Artificial lights are also excellent for raising seedlings.

TYPES OF LIGHTING

Incandescent light, produced by the familiar electric light bulb, is not suitable for growing vegetables when used as the sole source of light. In the first place it produces relatively little light for a given amount of electrical energy (measured in watts). More than 90% of the energy is converted to heat, which is not only wasteful but may actually damage the plants if they are not protected from the bulbs by, say, a sheet of glass. Fluorescent tubes, on the other hand, convert a much higher percentage of their energy into light, making them more economical and cooler-running. The lamps can be brought nearer the plants without risk of scorching the leaves, and so increase the intensity of light that they receive (although, of course, the closer to the plants, the fewer that can be covered). Fluorescents are fairly inexpensive, easy to obtain, simple to install, come in various lengths and will outlive any incandescent. Fluorescent tubes can last as long as 10,000 hours, compared with 1000 incandescent hours, although both lose light output as they age (and a fluorescent should be changed after a year's continuous use at around 16 hours a day, even though it still may appear as bright).

Plants cannot 'see' all the colours in white light, which vary from around 400nm (nanometers) in the violet range, to over 700nm in the red range of the spectrum.* The human eye, for example, responds greatly to green-yellow light, but plants have the least response to light in this range, and in fact reflect it. That's why they look green. Plants respond most to the colour waves towards the far end of the spectrum, the vital waves being the blue (at around 450nm), the red (650-700) and the far red (730), the latter being partly invisible to the naked eye.

While vegetables do not require sunlight *per se*, they should be provided with lights that offer the right sort of wavelength or colour balance. You must therefore know the spectrum produced by the various types of lights before installing them in your artificial light arrangement, otherwise your vegetables will not grow well.

As far as the colour balance of incandescents is concerned, they produce sufficient red and far red wavelengths, vital for the production of stems, roots and flowering processes, and in roughly the same proportion as sunlight, but they produce very little blue light, which is necessary for general development and particularly leaf growth and photosynthesis.

On the other hand, recent research has shown that however bright your fluorescent tubes may be they are not a complete substitute for sunlight. Their blue and red rays are usually sufficient, but their far red contribution is poor.

There are three possible solutions. You could go ahead and use ordinary fluorescents but avoid

*the nanometer is the currently accepted unit for measuring the length of light waves. One nm is one thousand millionth of a meter $(10 - 9m)$. Two other terms are also used: Angström (ten units A° equals one nm) and millimicrons (the equivalent to a nm).

growing any vegetables that flower and fruit, and preferably use such a set-up as a supplement to poor daylight which would still produce the necessary far red waves. Cool white and warm white tubes are a better choice than daylight or ordinary white.

Alternatively combine fluorescents with incandescents in the same lighting set-up to make up for each other's deficiencies. A ratio of 1:3 is widely recommended, say two 15 watt incandescents to two 40 watt fluorescent tubes. You will still have to face the problem of protecting the vegetables from the heat given off by the incandescents, although it will be spread over a wider area if you use two or more bulbs or low wattage instead of one more powerful bulb. Fruiting vegetables would receive their far red wavelengths necessary for flowering and fruiting (although you are unlikely to grow them to full maturity under artificial lighting anyway on account of their size, the problems of even-illumination, and the greater intensity of light they require compared with leafy and root crops. And bear in mind that other vegetables, lettuce for instance, may not need far red incandescent lighting as it tends to cause bolting [sending up a seed head] or flowering).

The final, and probably wisest, choice of lighting would be to buy the latest fluorescent tubes that have been developed by scientists specifically for horticultural purposes. They have names like True Lite, Plant Lite, Plant Gro, Gro Lux and so on. Their light is made up of a balance of blue, red and far red wavelengths that plants need, with less energy put into the yellow-green area. They do not, therefore, need to be used in conjunction with incandescents.

YOUR ARTIFICIAL LIGHTING

Any artificial light arrangement should be designed so that it can be raised above the plants as they grow, or the plants themselves should be capable of being raised to maintain close contact with the light

63

source. This can be done in a number of ways.

If you are using artificial lighting merely as a supplement to an area that receives inadequate natural light, the lamps could be suspended from the ceiling, or brackets, above a window and adjusted by a system of ropes, chains and/or pulleys. If the unit is to operate independently of natural light you could use adjustable shelving units. If the plants themselves are housed in individual pots their growing tips should be kept at the same level by standing the shorter ones on small boxes, blocks of wood or bricks, or the lighting can be sloped at an angle so that all the plants are kept in close contact with the light source.

Always use a reflector to concentrate the light output onto the plants. Make one yourself and paint it in reflective white or aluminium paint, or use tin foil. Thirty degrees is reckoned to be the optimum angle of light. Should the vegetables you decide to grow reach a height of over a foot, make roller blinds out of white PVC to fit round the sides of the growing area to further reflect light (look at the section in the book on making an automatic grow-box). They will also help to maintain a humid atmosphere within the unit.

When artificial lights are being used in conjunction with natural daylight make sure the reflector does not block out the latter. A removable reflector might be the answer, putting it and the lights on during the evenings.

Experiments in the United States have shown that soybeans and corn grown under artificial lights increase their yields by as much as a third when the surface of their growing compost was 'mulched', or covered, with tin foil that reflected light upwards thereby 'recycling' it to the plants from below. You might like to try it for yourself.

There are an increasing number of 'grow-units' manufactured for artificial light horticulture, but you could really make your own without too much trouble or expert carpentry skills. The easiest way would be to convert an old cabinet, refrigerator, radiogram, TV console, a cup board under, or above,

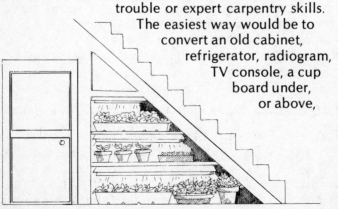

a sink, under the stairs, bookcases, an unused fireplace, room divider, and so on, to a growing space. Paint all inside surfaces white to reflect the light, and always keep both the surfaces, and the lamps themselves, super clean for maximum light, or else the object of the exercise will be lost.

Consider attics, cellars, garages, stairwells and other dim corners. Since they are likely to be cooler than the living room, and given the interdependence of light and temperature, the vegetables grown there would need less light intensity than those growing in a 70°F room. Position the units at eye level if you can, both for convenience of working and in order to actually see the crops behind their reflectors without wearing your knees out.

If you don't know what you're about as far as electricity is concerned, have the whole set-up installed by a qualified electrician. Never overload your supply circuit and even with fluorescents make sure you don't overheat anything. Always use grounded or earthed three core wire. And since there will be a lot of water around, use waterproof cables and fittings.

THE DURATION OF LIGHT (THE 'PHOTO PERIOD')

The rate of growth of your plants will be affected not only by the intensity of the light, the number and power of the lamps used and the distance they are from the plants, but also the length of time during the day in which they actually receive light.

So if your vegetables grow poorly through light starvation but you are unable to increase light intensity, the obvious solution would be to lengthen their artificial day.

Since artificial lights are less intense than natural light you should certainly leave the lamps on for longer than the day-light day. But while vegetables supposedly enjoy as long an artificial day as possible to stimulate their growth, in practice all vegetables do like a rest period.

Although the response of individual vegetables to the length of day and night, known as photoperiodism, will vary from vegetable to vegetable, none will grow well in continuous light.

During the night plants cease to photosynthesise and the process of taking in carbon dioxide and giving off oxygen are reversed. In fact plants do not 'rest' at night but rather spend the hours of darkness using up the food manufactured during the day in order to grow. The dark period in relation to day-length is also crucial in controlling other physiological processes, including flowering. Like people, plants must grow to a certain stage before they are able to reproduce. For many, a regulating factor in the time required to reach maturity is the length of days and nights. As far as indoor farming is concerned, there is an obvious danger that in your eagerness to encourage rapid growth you may give your vegetables too much light which can trigger off their reproductive functions and, say, cause early bolting in a winter lettuce. Or the reverse may happen and the vegetables that you want to flower will not do so because the dark period is of incorrect duration.

Most vegetables grow best if they receive a maximum of 16 hours' light a day and are allowed 8 hours of rest in total darkness. In winter the day-length should be between 12 and 14 hours. You will have to juggle around with these times and, by a process of trial and error, get the timings right and suitable to your own arrangement with regard to the intensity of available light, as well as other factors such as temperature and humidity.

Use an automatic timer on the lighting circuit and make certain that the vegetables are not subjected to the light from any source during their dark period as that could, however weak the bulb or brief the light, upset their growth. You cannot be expected to change your living pattern to suit your vegetables so precisely, but if you are using artificial lights in a growing area or room set aside for the purpose, it would be a good idea to use a green bulb as plants are not so responsive to that colour wavelength.

The costs of operating artificial lights in your indoor farm are really not excessive, especially in relation to the electrical energy we waste through the use of unnecessary appliances and gadgets, or perhaps leaving the television on long after everyone has lost interest in the programmes, or even the domestic use of the more inefficient incandescent bulbs instead of fluorescents. Compare the actual cost of your horticultural consumption of power to any other hobby — is it any more extravagant? Two 4 foot 40 watt fluorescent tubes would cost about two pence per full 16-hour working day. Measure that against the cost of buying winter salads from the shops, many of which will in fact have been commercially propagated under artificial light.

Automatic watering methods

Most vegetables will be able to survive without you for a weekend if you water them well before setting off and see to them the minute you open the door on your return. For longer periods away, two or three week summer holidays for example, a limited number could be taken care of by a good friend or neighbour especially on a 'you do mine and I'll do yours' basis. Without either you would be able to nurse potted vegetables through your absence by watering them well beforehand and covering them with polythene bags, using dry cleaner's bags for the largest ones. Blow them up and out, support them with canes so that they do not come into contact with the foliage, and tie them underneath the pot so that the plant is completely enclosed. The vegetables will still need light but protect them from direct sunlight, and the risks of being cooked in their plastic cocoon, with a shading of muslin or cheesecloth over the windows.

If the size of your indoor farm is relatively large, or if you take frequent or long holidays, or if your memory isn't particularly good, you ought to consider installing automatic watering methods. They are essential if you plan on employing other automated growing techniques, such as thermostatic heating or time-switch artificial lighting, otherwise the advantages of having the latter are somewhat lost. Automatic watering is an almost essential aspect of hydroponic cultivation too. The following suggestions range in scale from individual pot to grandiose self-watering beds. You will easily be able to model an in-between arrangement to satisfy your own requirements.

Various types of self-watering 'fill and forget' pots are now widely available from garden centres and plant shops, designed to take some of the guesswork and headaches out of watering. They are made for house plants but are perfectly suited to any vegetables that will fit the particular size of pot, (the range of which includes self-watering hanging baskets). Most have an outer reservoir that has to be kept topped up (with plain water, occasionally diluted fertiliser, or hydroponic nutrient solution). Others utilise a funnel device which is stuck into the compost, or into a porous material surrounding the pot. One such version comprises a porous earthenware cone that is soaked in water and placed in the compost with a tube connecting it to a container of water that replenishes the liquid as it is absorbed by the plant.

Single pot, wick-feed arrangements are easy to set up. Football boot laces, nylon, cheesecloth or specially made fibre matting can be used for the wick. One end is threaded into the pot's drainage hole, unravelled and spread out over the bottom of the pot, while the other end is placed in a container of water below the level of the pot. Moisten the wick first and, as the roots draw water from the soil round them, it is replaced by 'capillary' action from the reservoir. Never crock the drainage holes in the pots if you are using any of the capillary watering methods.

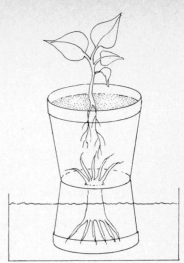

A group of pots (or seed trays with drainage holes) can be automatically watered by the 'wet blanket' method. Buy a convenient size of capillary fibre matting which, if kept in continuous contact with a supply of water, will provide water for the plants standing on the mat, and also help provide a humid atmosphere in their immediate vicinity. First put down a sheet of plastic on your growing table, slightly larger than the size of the matting. Make sure that the surface is absolutely level or the water will not reach all the pots in equal proportion.

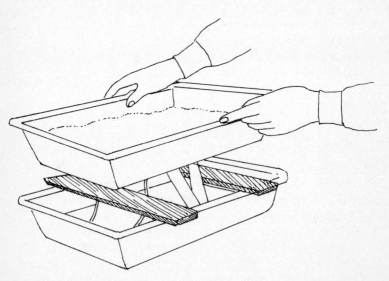

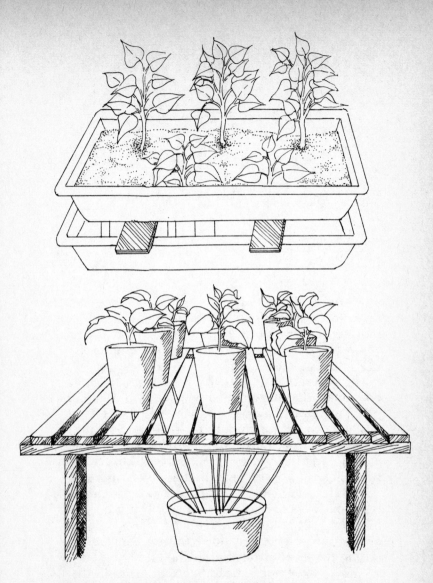

Soak the matting in water and lightly wring out any excess before placing it in position on the sheet. One end of the mat should be draped into a water reservoir, a roasting tin for example, or the mat may come ready supplied with its own reservoir and level control unit.

Moisten the compost well in each of the pots before standing them on the matting and leave capillary action to do the work. As the roots absorb

moisture it will be drawn up through the drainage holes from the matting which, in turn, will draw on the supply of water in the reservoir. The mat itself will retain quite a bit of water, about a gallon for every square yard.

The vegetables growing from the pots, or other containers that have drainage holes, will drink up as much water as they need, leaving you free of anxieties about the amount or frequency of watering. If you think that a particular vegetable is getting more than it really needs, for example a pot of garlic that should never be too moist, move the pot to the end of the mat furthest away from the reservoir, where the water supply will still be constant, but at a slightly reduced rate. A smaller amount of water absorption can be achieved by raising the level of the mat at the far end by an inch or two — experiment with the exact level till the moisture touch seems about right. To conserve moisture, cover the capillary matting with black polythene and cut out holes where the pots are to stand.

The only non-automatic aspect of these capillary water systems is to make sure that the reservoir is kept topped up. The larger the reservoir, the longer it will keep going without your help. A one-gallon container should be enough to supply a 10 to 15 square foot mat filled with pots, in fairly warm conditions, for a day. For larger areas, or longer periods, you must increase the size of the water container. Use a bucket, an inverted demi-john, or similar container and stand it at least a couple of feet above the level of the matting to give sufficient head pressure to supply the matting. Capillary matting kits usually come ready supplied with tubing and a suitable valved connecter to join the supply tank to the feeder tray. Otherwise make your own connection in the way described below. Put a lid, if necessary, over the supply tank to prevent the water evaporating before it has done its job, and keep dust out of the supply. It is also a good idea to protect glass tanks from the light as algae may develop and block the connecting valve. Any such reservoir can, of course, be filled with nutrient solution, instead of plain water, for hydroponic cultivation.

Your 'water bed' can be left completely unattended, at least as far as watering is concerned, for an indefinite period if the water supply is connected to the mains water via a valve-controlled cistern, just like the familiar lavatory. The actual supply of water can be more precisely monitored by an electromagnetic water-valve, connected to a small photo-electric cell that reacts according to the amount of solar energy present. But it will be difficult to supply hydroponic nutrients as part of this since mains water is not endowed with the necessary chemicals.

Sand, the coarse builders sort, can be used as a substitute for capillary matting with the advantage that it is cheaper to buy; the disadvantage is its weight and general messiness. You can make a self-watering bench for your indoor farm, tailor-made to fit into a convenient area such as an awkward-shaped bay window.

Draw up the measurements for the bench and cut the base to size from ¾ inch chipboard. The sides should be made from 3 by 2 inch softwood. Nail them to the base and to each other. Line the bench with heavy duty polythene and secure it to the top of the side pieces with battens. Cover the base with a ½ inch layer of gravel. Water can be supplied by one of two methods, either by a length of flexible plastic pipe running along the length of the bench and perforated with holes (through which the water will leak out), or press a flower pot into the gravel so that it comes into contact with the base of the bench, at the same end where you plan to secure the water reservoir.

Cover the bottom of the bench with 2 inches of sand or ½ an inch of gravel and 1½ inches of sand (the depth of the sand can be changed to increase or decrease the degree of watering if it proves too much or too little). Again check to make certain that the whole arrangement is on the level. The pots should be twisted into the sand and should not have their drainage holes crocked.

The perforated pipe should be connected up to an easily-obtained valve device which will regulate the flow of water from the reservoir, be it hand-filled, header-tank, or mains-connected. Moisten the compost in the pots well before 'switching on'.

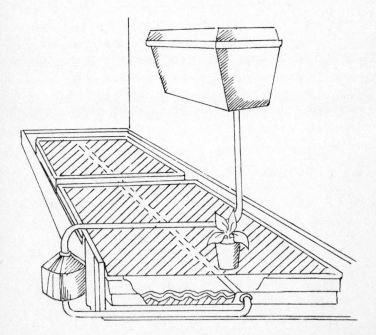

With the flower-pot method, soak the sand with water until it reaches half inch deep in the bottom of the flower pot. Push a short length of glass tube through an already holed cord (a winemaker's supplier will have one), attach a length of tight-fitting rubber tube to the glass tube, fill the jar with water, turn upside down, support it, and position the tube so that it is suspended in the flower pot ½ an inch above its base. In other words, the end of the tube is at the same level as that of the water in the bench. As the water is drawn up by the plants, and therefore sinks in the flower pot, water will be released from the jar and down the tube. As long as the jar contains water, the level at the base of the watering bench will always remain at ½ inch. The jar itself must be held above the bench by means of a wooden bracket arrangement. The diagram will

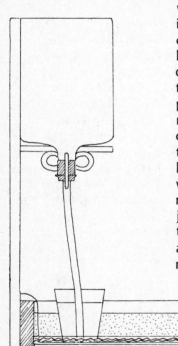

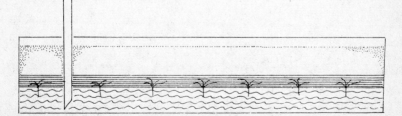

make all this much clearer than it sounds. It's actually quite simple to construct. Honestly.

The other diagram shows an easy to make, automatically-watered window box. It is fitted with a 2 inch deep false bottom, which acts as the water reservoir, and wicks pass through holes into the water, Their tops are spread out in a ½ inch layer of sand. The filler tube is made from ¾ inch plastic hose, cutaway at the bottom as the diagram shows.

The second basic system of automatic watering is known as drip, or trickle, irrigation. On a small scale, a one-pot-to-one-water-container relationship, use a plastic jar and cut a small semi-hole out of the rim. It should be large enough for a piece of glass capillary tube or similar size length of plastic tubing to fit snugly. If you use glass tubing, for greater accuracy of drip, bend it in two places over a gas flame in the way you learnt in science at school and have probably forgotten, so that it makes the shape shown in the diagram (and otherwise indescribable). Plastic tubing should be manipulated to roughly the same shape in the final set-up.

Fill the jar with water (or hydroponic nutrient solution), place a dish over the mouth and turn the

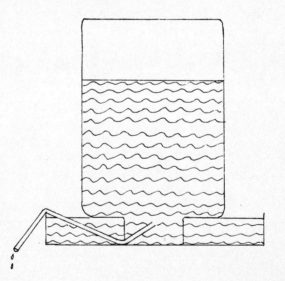

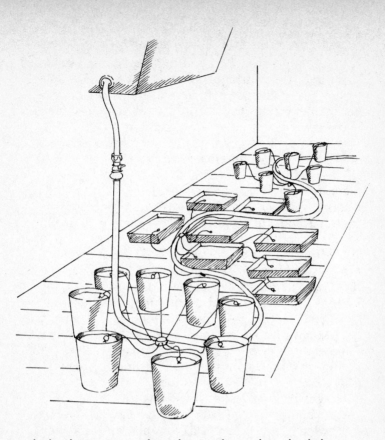

whole thing over. After the applause has died down you will notice that some of the water has gone into the dish. Stick one end of the tube into the hole in the jar's rim and the other end can be trained to drip wherever you want it to. The rate of drip can be altered by raising or lowering the slope of the tube.

Larger watering systems can be built using the same principle. A large tube is connected to a tap and the overall rate of water flow can be adjusted by turning the tap. From the main tube several feeder tubes are attached, linking the water supply to individual pots or boxes. At the end of each is a nozzle so that each pot can have its own personal drip rate to suit whatever happens to be growing there. Once again the water supply can be from the mains or replenished manually.

Hydroponics

If you are enthusiastic about indoor farming in spirit, but are a little put off by the dread of having to lug heavy bags of compost all the way from the garden centre, up to the top of a multi-storey block, and then across the living-room carpet, think hydroponically. You can do without compost or soil altogether. Your containers can all be filled with a feather-light aggregate and your crops will grow magnificently if you just water them with life-giving potions. And virtually any crop can be grown by such methods, in more or less the same way as you would for ordinary cultivation.

Hydroponics, also known as soil-less or chemi-culture, has had an enormous impact on the developing countries in the world where the soil is either too poor for food production, or there is no soil at all. It is also an ideal method of cultivation for people without gardens, and for those who just have a patch of builder's rubble outside; hydroponics can convert even that into a vegetable plot.

How is it possible to do away with soil, or some sort of compost? Soil performs two key functions for a growing plant. It serves as an anchor, supporting the roots of the plant to keep it standing in the right position. It is also a source of vital nutrients that plants need to feed on. Hydroponic methods use alternative materials, or aggregates, to hold the plant in position, while it is fed with a nutrient solution that contains all the minerals, correctly balanced in the right proportions, to sustain growth. These minerals are dissolved in water and fed to the plant just as you might water them in the ordinary way.

Since hydroponic cultivation is far superior to compost growing it is remarkable that the method hasn't achieved greater popularity with all gardeners, especially house-plant rearers and budding farmers. In the first place, there is absolutely no risk of the soil being deficient in the minerals needed by growing plants or there being too much of some nutrients that would upset their balanced development, since you will provide all these requirements. There can be no soil-borne diseases or weeds since the growing medium is inert. Unlike composts it will never need to be enriched or replaced, nor will you have to dig, rotate your crops as you would in a garden, or rake and aerate the soil. The surface will never cake or pan down, and so cause unhealthy roots and the eventual souring of the compost. All your work will be cleaner and easier. This is beginning to sound like the lazy farmer's dream.

On top of all these advantages you will be able to exercise much better control over your growing crops. The vegetables will be more uniform in appearance and quicker to mature. Since they can be planted closer together — they won't have to compete for the nutrients in ordinary soil or compost — their yields will be more buxom in relation to the space they occupy. By the same token they will not need to be housed in such deep containers as the roots will not have to dig so profoundly to find their food. In sum, your hydroponically raised crops will be better in quality and quantity since it is a more accurate system of cultivation in which optimum growing conditions can be more easily achieved.

As far as the nutrients are concerned, you do not have to be a chemistry genius before starting a hydroponic farming unit. On a domestic, as opposed to commercial, scale it will be wiser to buy ready mixed compounds that are sold by most of the larger horticultural suppliers and seedsmen. These powders, or sometimes tablets, contain all that your vegetables need to sustain growth—nitrogen, phosphorus, potassium, calcium, magnesium, sulphur, iron, plus essential trace elements. All you have to do is mix them with water. If you do find that your scale of farming increases it will save money if you mix up your own from basic ingredients. You will also be able to play around with their proportions to suit the requirements of individual vegetables (leaf crops, for example, prefer more nitrogen, vegetable crops more potassium, roots more phosphorus, and so on). But don't bother to do this in the beginning since the ready-mixed chemicals work out inexpensive, and there is never any waste since you only supply the precise needs of the vegetables.

The compound powder should be dissolved and stirred into water, following the manufacturer's instructions for the correct mixing ratio (about one teaspoonful to two gallons of water, but this can vary from chemical to chemical). Make a weaker solution for young seedlings or vegetables growing in poor light conditions, and a stronger dose for vegetables in their prime of life in the middle of summer.

You can use different types of aggregate to support the vegetables. The word hydroponics literally means 'water culture', a method by which the roots of plants are directly suspended in the nutrient solution. We will not go into this particular method as it is rather tricky to set up and not really practical for non-commercial growers.

Sand or vermiculite are most commonly used, and often mixed together (2 parts sand to 3 vermiculite). Use coarse builder's sand and check there is no lime in it, in the shape of sea shell fragments perhaps, as this would upset the nutrient balance. Never use sea-side sand as the salt residue is likely to prove harmful to the vegetables. Vermiculite is a substance that has been expanded by heat to form small granules. It is absorbent, sterile (with no risk of soil-born nasties), light in weight and attractive to look at. Buy special horticultural vermiculite, fairly easy to come by, though often sold under varying trade names. You can also use gravel, small pebbles, washed cinders and a few other things, but sand and vermiculite are best. If you choose sand you can prevent unsightly, but harmless algae forming on the moist surface by covering it with a layer of small pebbles or granite chips.

Look at the suggestions on p. 35-8 for containers. Basically anything will do as long as it holds water, and is at least 6 inches deep. The container should have drainage holes that can be plugged with cork, plasticine or chewing gum. These are most conveniently located at one end with the other end propped up slightly with a thin strip of wood or cotton bobbins. Crock in the usual way (unless you are going to use sub-irrigation/capillary automatic watering systems — see automatic watering) with pieces of broken flower pot or use nylon gauze.

Growing vegetables in a hydroponic unit is essentially the same as cultivation in any sort of container. Before sowing your seeds moisten the medium so that water begins to run freely from the drainage holes. Leave it to drain. Sow the seeds in the usual way, bearing in mind that vegetables grown hydroponically can be spaced closer together than is normally the case provided they get plenty of light. Summer sowings, for instance, can be closer than those in winter.

After sowing the seeds sprinkle the aggregate with plain water but do not firm then down as you would in compost. Keep the aggregate as moist as a wrung-out sponge. Twenty-four hours after sowing give the seeds their first feed with nutrient solution. Start with the mixture at half strength and gradually increase to full strength after the seeds have germinated. Reduce the strength of the solution during times of slow growth, usually in the winter months.

If you are planting seedlings bought from a nursery, or mail-order supplier, you must very gently wash away all traces of soil or compost adhering to

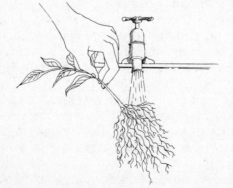

the roots before planting in the hydroponic unit;
otherwise you risk spreading soil-borne disease and
upsetting the nutrient balance. When transplanting
from vermiculite or sand (as opposed to compost or
soil) to vermiculite or sand, remove the seedlings
with a fork so that a clump of the aggregate remains
around the established root system. This will provide
a continuing moisture and nutrient supply, and so
minimise the shock to the plant. Hydroponically-
grown vegetables will need repotting less than
compost-raised crops because the nutrients and
water they need are more conveniently obtained by
the root system. Stakes for taller vegetables grown,
in vermiculite should be attached to the outside of
the container since the aggregate is not rigid enough
to hold them upright.

The simplest way to water/feed your vegetables is
from overhead with a fine rose-headed watering can,
just like watering plants in the ordinary way. Keep
the aggregate moist and never overwater because
this can prevent air reaching the roots and cause
them to rot. You will find that sand will need more
liquid than porous vermiculite. Use either a fresh
solution of nutrient each time, or re-cycle the old by
catching it as it comes through the drainage holes.
Change the solution once a week and at the same
time allow the container to thoroughly drain.
Draining and refilling causes air to move in and out
of the aggregate and reach the roots. Once every
ten days or so you should flush the aggregate out
with plain water to remove any accumulation of
mineral salts that may turn sour.

As an alternative to overhead watering, the
individual pots can be half submerged in a container
of nutrient solution which is soaked up through the
aggregate to the roots of the vegetable by capillary
action, and then, after about half an hour, allowed
to drain back into the reservoir. As the liquid drains
out the air in the aggregate is replaced by fresh air.
Larger arrangements can be 'sub-irrigated' in this
way by a gravity-feed system along the lines of the
one shown in the drawing. The inlet pipe is secured
to the holes in both containers by nuts and epoxy

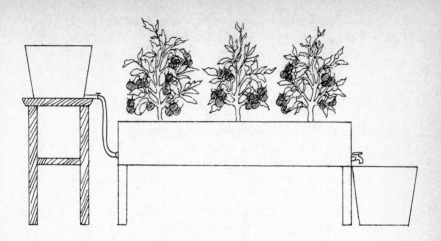

resin. Raise the bucket in the morning to feed and
lower in the evening so that it can be drained
overnight. The vegetable container should slope
towards the feeding hole. Keep the nutrient reservoir
topped up and covered to prevent losses due to
evaporation. If the aggregate seems to be too wet or
too dry vary the interval between feeding and
draining. This method works best with gravel, and
not so brilliantly with vermiculite.

The larger the container of vegetables, the larger
the nutrient reservoir that will be needed, and the
larger the biceps you will require to lift it up and
down. If you lack the strength or inclination, use a

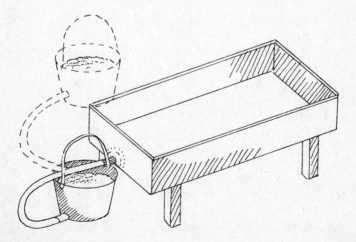

system of pulleys to ease the load or operate the
sub-irrigation system with a small electric pump
connected to a time switch. The nutrient solution
can then be automatically pumped into the
vegetable container at intervals of time that are pre-
selected according to the weather, temperature,
stage of growth and type of vegetable. Between
pumping times the solution drains back into its
reservoir ready for the next pumping cycle. Start off
with a two-hour-a-day pumping operation, and
moderate it one way or the other depending on how
everything goes.

The electric pump system of feeding will also be a
great advantage whenever you want to get away
from your indoor farm for a few days, or for an
automated set-up that you may want to construct.
The automatic watering methods that are dealt with
in the last chapter can easily be adapted to
hydroponic culture. Since the water contains
dissolved minerals you will have to make provision
for draining out the system and washing with plain
water about every ten days to two weeks. If you do
flush out the aggregate regularly, and smooth it over
when you replant or re-sow your vegetables, you can
use the aggregate again and again.

Farming in a spare room

There may be a spare room in your home that is
employed merely as a catch-all for the odds and
ends that don't seem to belong to any other place, a
sort of junk purgatory for those once-useful objects
before they reach the dustbin. If they could be
found homes elsewhere, or at least tucked away into
one corner, it could be the first step in the
establishment of a room farm. Any spare room has a
great deal of potential for the successful conversion
into a flourishing food farm. But before you start
digging in, consider how the overall structure of the
room could be best adapted to the concept.

All wall, ceiling, and floor surfaces if possible,
should be painted in a reflective white paint so as to

84

maximise the amount of light available within the
room. Beyond that there are two other ways of
increasing the amount of light available to the
crops: you could either add to or enlarge the
existing glazed areas, or install an intensive artificial
lighting arrangement. Or both.

Nowadays the replacement of south-facing roof
expanses with solar energy panels has become all
the ecological rage. But the much less expensive
concept of replacing tiles with glass, thereby turning
an unused attic or loft area into a well-illuminated
space for food growing, is rarely considered. Surely
the economic gains from either system of using the
sun can be favourably compared.

A loft can be brightened up by a skylight made of
reinforced glass for safety's sake, running the whole
(south facing if possible) side of the roof. It should
be double-glazed to keep the heating bill down in
winter, and to insulate against excessive summer
heat. If you use white fibreglass for the double-
glazing it will also act as a filter against strong
direct sunlight. A large dormer window, or a picture
window in a wall of the house, would provide a
much more limited area of light intensity for plant
growth; but if the plants are cleverly arranged to get
all the light that's going you would be able to grow
a significant amount of food for each additional
area of wall or roof space that you convert to glass.
Those areas that don't receive natural light can, of
course, be illuminated by artificial lighting, or used
to grow foods that will thrive in the dark, such as
sprouting seeds, mushrooms and some forced
vegetables.

Such conversions, if done purely to create
suitable growing space, would constitute a major
investment and the outlay could only be justified
over many years of eating. Apart from installing
windows, the joists will probably need strengthening
as they are likely to be designed merely to support
the ceiling below not the burden of tubs filled with
potting compost. And most loft areas would need
flooring laid across the joists, or you would
constantly risk appearing through the ceiling of the

room below. But if it is to be regarded as a pleasure, as well as a source of other non-monetary advantages gained from enjoying home-grown food, the costs should certainly be considered in relation to these joys, just as you would before buying, say, a camera, a set of golf clubs or a hi-fi system.

Home extensions, similarly, are highly suitable for indoor farming, so don't ever feel that adding one to your house implies cutting back on your backyard or garden growing resources. The square footage within the home extension will be much more productive than its outdoor equivalent. And it is more than feasible for such a room to be devoted to growing vegetables and yet still continue to function as part of your home's living area.

The Victorian enthusiasm for conservatories, in which exotic foliages were created, can thrive again in the modern sun lounge. Pre-fabricated or do-it-yourself, they are easily erected and are light, bright constructions that will please plants and people.

Both will flourish — in fact you'll bring carbon dioxide and they'll supply oxygen-rich air, a rare treat in today's cities.

Choose an extension that has plenty of window area and a translucent roof. Glass looks better, and will last longer than plastic, but the roof will have to be reinforced with wire netting (otherwise it could prove dangerous if something were to fall on the glass — even a chunk of snow from the roof could shatter it). The roof should also slope to prevent leaves and such-like from blocking out your light, and to allow winter condensation to run off. A double layer of glass or plastic will also help prevent condensation, as well as insulate the atmosphere inside, thereby lessening temperature extremes and keeping your heating bills down.

Try to locate the extension so that it faces south, or as south-to-south-west as you can make it, with doors leading outside as well as into the house, for convenience. Don't equip the room with the usual range of furniture and carpets because the atmosphere will soon be their ruin. In fact, whatever place in the home you decide to devote to indoor farming on a fairly intensive scale, make all flooring

waterproof, using vinyl or ceramic tiles, so that any
upset watering cans don't leave their mark on either
carpeting or the ceiling below. Any exposed timbers
should be well protected against both spillage and
humidity by non-creosote wood-preservative topped

off with white reflective paint. Electric wiring should be moisture proof and preferably installed by an expert. Or you can buy specially pre-wired greenhouse kits that need only one connection to the mains.

All growing rooms should be made as snug and draught-proof as possible, insulated against the vagaries of an outdoor winter, and yet able to be ventilated to create the buoyant atmosphere that growing things thrive in.

It would be convenient to have a water tap and sink in the room, or at least fairly accessible. Even the most devoted indoor farmer might find that his interest begins to wane if watering involved several up and down stair pilgrimages a day. In an attic you may have to install a small electric pump to raise the water above its 'head' if the house is not connected to a rising main. If you plan to automate your growing room, then mains water supply would be a great advantage. This would then operate in conjunction with automatic watering, controlled ventilation, thermostatically regulated heat (with greenhouse fan heater perhaps, or an extension radiator linked to the existing system although heat loss from the lower rooms may be sufficient provided the roof itself is insulated), provision for humidifying the atmosphere, and some method of shading against scorching sunlight. Although initially quite expensive to set up, automated systems mean greater control over the vegetables' growing environment, less time devoted to their routine looking-after, and the opportunity to get away from it all.

Making an automatic grow-box

You could build a grow-box that will automatically provide the right conditions needed to sustain a crop of vegetables entirely independent of the environment in the home. It would require only a minimum of attention once every couple of weeks. Such a grow-box, or 'green' box is, in effect, a

controlled microclimate, better than nature can
offer, in which vegetables will grow to perfection,
even enabling you to harvest fresh salads for
Christmas lunch. It will also be stimulating as an on-
going experiment for children to observe how plants
grow.

Technically it is possible to provide artificially the
perfect conditions to grow virtually any plant known
to man, no matter in which climatic region of the
world it grows naturally. But a green box for home
vegetable production need not be as complicated a
piece of equipment, and certainly nowhere near as
precision-built, as the growth chambers that are
used in experimental horticulture to measure the
effects on plants of minute variations in one
variable while others are held absolutely constant.

If you use an old aquarium, or make a 'terrarium'
out of a wooden frame structure covered in clear
plastic, it can be positioned so that the plants
receive all their fill of natural light. Otherwise you
will need to construct an artificial lighting
arrangement as described in the earlier chapter. If
you build a box, rather than convert an existing
cupboard, its overall measurements should be
decided by the length of the fluorescent tubes —
either 4 or 8 foot long would be most suitable, and
a width of 2 feet would allow four tubes to be
housed side by side.

The base of the box should be tray-shaped, the base made from ½ inch thick chipboard, and the sides out of 3 by 2 inch (planed) timber. Screw the side edges together and glue and screw them to the base. Seal the joining edges with a liquid seal (or screw and glue with waterproof glue) as an extra precaution against leaks, and line the box with heavy duty polythene. Drill a row of ½ or ¾ inch holes along one narrow end and fit them with corks.

Make the uprights out of 2 by 1 inch wood and secure each one to the ends of the tray with two bolts. Before assembling, drill a series of evenly-spaced ¼ inch holes all along the four uprights.

The top of the box, which will provide support for the lamps, can be made from hardboard or plywood mounted on a frame of 1 inch square wood battens, fixed together as the diagram shows so that the corners will fit over the four uprights. The top can be supported by 4 ¼ inch dowels so that the height of the lights can be adjusted and kept at the same distance above the plants as they grow.

Before fixing the tubes to the top support, paint the underside, and any other inside surfaces of a converted box, with a highly reflective white or aluminium paint. This will reflect and scatter light giving more-uniform illumination than, say, mirror tiles or tin foil. The top can have side flaps to reflect light down onto the plants or, better still, you can surround the entire box with white PVC curtains, with their shiny side facing inwards. They can be mounted on rollers on the sides of the tray and attached to the top by hooks so that they will be pulled up with the top as its height is re-adjusted. The enclosed nature of the box will also help maintain an environment high in humidity as it will retain moisture evaporated from the sand, compost or capillary matting used as a growing base, and transpired by the plants. Don't make it airtight however as the vegetables will suffer without adequate ventilation.

If you want the green box to be heated during the winter independently of room temperature, install

soil-warming cables or air-warming cables if you are
using a capillary mat, around the inside of the base
tray. The manufacturer's instructions will explain
how. Both soil- and air-warming cables can be
regulated by a thermostat. Water, or rather a
hydroponic mineral solution, can be fed to the tray
by any of the automatic watering methods already
mentioned.

The final stage in the assembly of the box is to
link the lighting circuit to the mains via a time-clock
so that it will switch on and off according to a pre-
arranged programme.

Your job will be to keep the nutrient solution
topped up, and to flush out the box every so often,
and to raise the roof as the vegetables grow taller.

Part Two
GETTING GOING

Tools for indoor farming

Somewhere in your urban environment, before you
convert every nook and cranny to farming, you
should set aside a small cupboard for storing all
your pots, seed packets, odds and ends, and your
tools.

Indoor farmers won't need nearly as much in the
way of basic equipment as your outdoor
counterparts. Gardening stores are filled with all
sorts of tools, many of which are unnecessary
gadgets, no matter what the scale of farming you
are able to undertake. They are a complete waste of
money. Who needs to buy plant labels with lolly-
sucking kids around?

But never try to save money by buying poor
quality tools. The well-known brands fully warrant
the extra money spent on them as they will outlive
less expensive substitutes many times over. Look
after them. Wash and clean them with a rag after
use and wipe with an oily rag before putting them
away for any length of time.

Even the basic tools needed for indoor farming
can be improvised from household objects, although
in the long run the right tool for the right job will
always be the wisest policy.

The basic tools you will need are:
  a hand trowel — the small type for indoor work
    (or use a kitchen spoon);
  a hand fork — again the small type (or kitchen
    fork);
  a small watering can, with a fine rose attachment.
    Buy a second can to be used solely for
    insecticides; never use one can for both;
  a fine water spray.
You will also need: string, scissors (or secateurs), a

penknife, an old cake knife and a metre cum feet and inches ruler. A moisture meter would make a welcome birthday present.

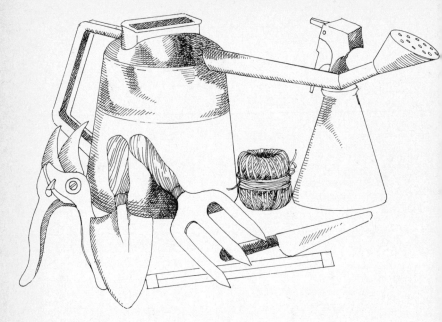

Raising vegetables from seed

It is both more economical and more satisfying to raise as many of your vegetables from seed as is practical. Send away for the seed catalogues from the major seedsmen and spend a few hours browsing through before deciding what to grow. The free catalogues are a mine of information on the different varieties of crops that are available to the amateur grower.

Once you have decided what you want, order the seeds early in the year before everyone else gets to them, either direct from the seedsman (fill in the order form that comes with the catalogue), or go to your local garden centre, nursery or chain store to see if they stock what you want. If you belong to a horticultural society or gardening club you may be able to buy seeds at discount rates, although for the indoor farmer the savings will be minimal. But it may be worth sharing seed packets with a neighbour as each one will contain more than you'll need for any one year.

Any left-over seeds should be stored in airtight tins in a cool, dark place. With a few exceptions most of them will keep for two or three years, although their germination rate is bound to fall off. Grain seeds found in the tombs of the Egyptian Pharaohs were still capable of germination . . .

Choose F.1 Hybrids where possible. These are raised by controlled fertilisation between two selected parents, and while such a pedigree tends to make them a little more expensive than the others, they generally produce a better and heavier crop. You cannot, however, save your own seeds from vegetables grown from F.1 Hybrids, although on the indoor farming scale of food growing you may not consider this worth it anyhow except for the sense of satisfaction that you get from doing so.

Raising vegetables from seed or propagation *indoors* makes sense even for those people who do have a garden or backyard, as well as those with patio or balcony space. It gives crops an early start to life so avoiding delays to sowing because of poor weather, and the plants will occupy the valuable outdoor area for a shorter time. Many vegetables stand a much better chance of germinating, or becoming seedlings, if sown indoors where the temperature can be controlled and sustained at a higher level. The seedlings, after this cosy and secure start to life, can be moved outside once the weather has warmed up. But some vegetables, particularly root crops, peas, spinach and others, must be sown in their final growing position, wherever that may be, because they don't take kindly to being moved around.

A few salad crops, and a limited range of herbs, are sold pre-planted in peat growing pots, housed in their own plastic mini-greenhouse or propagating top. Other seeds can be bought pre-sown in tubs, or grow-packs, filled with a dry growing-medium (such as vermiculite) and they will germinate as soon as water is added. But, as a rule, most vegetable seeds are propagated in the following way.

You can use either seed trays (make your own from fruit crates lined with tin foil or polythene), small pots, or a whole range of improvised containers (margarine tubs, yoghurt pots, plastic sandwich boxes, plastic cups, tin cans, aluminium pie-trays, plastic egg boxes [the tops will act as a greenhouse cover], cut off cardboard milk cartons and so on). Or you can use either peat pots or peat pellets. Whatever you decide to use the methods of propagation will all be roughly the same.

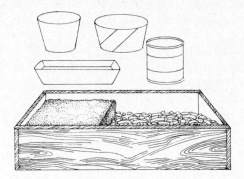

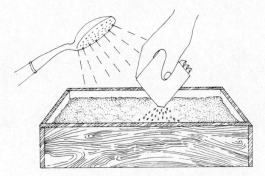

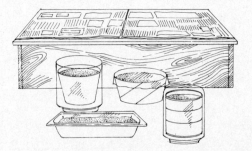

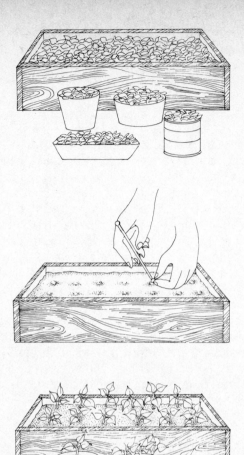

   If the container you are using doesn't have
drainage holes you must make them, using a knife, a
pair of pointed scissors or a hammer and nail. You
should also crock these drainage holes with pieces
of broken flower pot, china or small pebbles, to
prevent the compost from blocking the hole, or
escaping through it.
   Fill the container to within ¾ inch, roughly, of
the top with seed compost. The gap will give young

seedlings sprouting room and allow air to circulate. Buy a proprietary brand of seed compost, such as John Innes, as it is a specially prepared mix, sterilised to be weed-, pest- and disease-free so that anything that grows in it will be what you've planted. The texture is also ideal for the development of young plants. The standard John Innes formula for seed compost consists of two parts loam, one part peat, one part sharp sand, plus 1½ oz superphosphate and ¾ oz of lime per bushel.

Thoroughly moisten the compost, either by watering overhead or, better still, stand the container in shallow water in a bath or sink. Allow it to drain and press the surface down lightly.

Soak the larger seeds overnight, unless they are pelleted seeds, since their special coating, designed to make smaller seeds easier to handle and sow at their correct spacing, will dissolve in water. Sow the larger seeds in individual holes made in the compost with a pencil or knitting needle, two inches apart, or put two or three seeds into a three inch peat pot. Just press pelleted seeds into the surface and lightly cover with a little moist compost. Smaller seeds should be sprinkled evenly all over the surface and then covered with a fine layer of moist compost which is pressed down gently. The section in the book on individual vege- tables, as well as the seed packets, will tell you just how deeply each type should be sown, roughly two or three times their diameter. Peat pellets have to be watered and the peat will slowly expand to take the seed's developing root system.

Sow small quantities of each vegetable frequently, every ten days or so, rather than all at once. This technique, known as successional sowing, will avoid gluts and guarantee constant supplies throughout the growing season.

Label each container with the name of the vegetable, its variety and the date of sowing. Keep a written record of such information and make comments on the performance of the vegetables for future reference.

Cover each container with glass, polythene, plastic kitchen seal or a jam or sweet-jar, or use the purpose-built propagating tops that fit snugly over

their own seed trays. This will help retain moisture, maintain a snug temperature and create a favourably humid atmosphere. At this stage seeds are incapable of sucking up moisture as their roots have yet to develop. The moist atmosphere will soften the seed coat and trigger off germination.

Keep the containers in a warm and dim place (or cover with newspaper to keep out bright light). The compost should remain fairly moist, so water it from below should it become dry. But never let it become waterlogged as this can cause 'damping off', a fungal disease that can rot seeds before they germinate, or the stems of the tiny seedlings at soil level. Damping off can also be caused by poor drainage or excessive heat. Remove the covers once a day to ventilate the seedlings (or open up the ventilation holes on shop-bought propagators) and wipe away the condensation that forms on the inside of the glass.

The process of propagation is one of the most basic in nature. The moisture in the compost releases the embryo plant from the state of dormancy and it expands to rupture the seed coating. The seed contains food reserves which break down and sustain the plant for the first few days of its life. It will then develop a root system, which will anchor it in the compost and absorb both water and nutrients, and a shoot with green leaves that will be able to photosynthesise.

It is important to maintain the correct level of temperature during this propagation stage in the plant's life. It should be warm — most seeds need about 60-65 degrees day and night. If the temperature is too low they may well fail to germinate (although lettuces best germinate at a low temperature). If too high they will germinate too rapidly and emerge as weaklings, or the heat could kill them off completely (heat, after all, is the essence of sterilisation which destroys all weed-seeds).

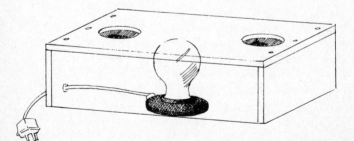

The best places for propagation are likely to be an airing cupboard, on a shelf above a radiator, or on top of an artificial light reflector. You could build a tiered unit of four or five seed trays, with those seeds requiring the highest temperature sown in the bottom tray, nearest the radiator shelf. Or build a hot stand out of a wooden box (an old drawer) and an incandescent bulb, with ventilation holes drilled in the sides as in the diagram.

The most controlled way to propagate seeds is to use a heated electric propagator with a thermostatic control. Either buy one, or make one yourself using soil- (and perhaps air-) warming cables as your heat source. They are not expensive to operate and are

mainly designed for use in a greenhouse so that the temperature inside the propagator can be kept at a constant high level without the cost of heating the entire greenhouse to that level. But they are a useful extra for indoor farming, especially if your central heating system switches off at night. Once bottom heat is no longer required the seedlings can be moved and replaced with a freshly sown seed tray so that a succession is maintained.

After the seedlings have germinated, and are poking their heads up out of the compost, they should be given more light. But wait until they have grown their second set of leaves before giving them full sunlight. These leaves are known as 'true' leaves, as opposed to the first two 'seed' leaves or 'cotyledons', that are the seed's food store. There are usually two, although onions send up only one, and cabbage four. A tin-foil reflector, placed behind the seedlings, will help them grow up straight, and prevent their becoming drawn and leggy.

Keep the seedlings moist but do not remove their glass covers until they reach the top of the seed tray. Then leave the top off for an hour or so the first day, increasing the amount of time daily until after four or five days they will be ready to face the world without a roof over their heads.

Once the first pair of true leaves looks well-established they can be thinned out wherever they begin to crowd each other, and before their roots become interwined. Either discard the extra ones or 'prick out', planting them 2 inches apart in another seed tray, or one to a 3 inch peat pot, to give them more room to grow. The new compost should be potting compost, again a proprietary brand such as John Innes, because its mix is coarser, better suited to the stage in the plants' life. Use grade No. 2.

Thoroughly moisten both composts before moving the seedlings. Make holes for the tiny roots with a pencil in the potting compost and lift the seedlings by the leaves, gently prising the roots free with a fork or spoon. Never pull, or even touch, the delicate stem. Lower the seedling carefully into its new home, gently firm down the compost and keep moist.

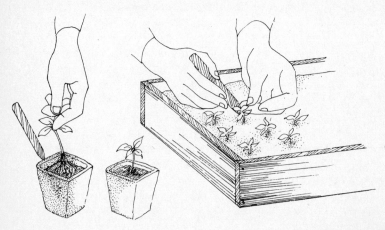

Transplanting

When the seedlings have grown two or three pairs of leaves, they will be ready for repotting or transplanting to their final growing position, be it pot, window sill, grow-bag or wherever. Use John Innes potting compost No. 3. The standard John Innes potting compost formula consists of 7 parts loam, 3 peat, 2 sharp sand, plus 4oz of 'J.I.' base and ¾ oz of chalk per bushel. The 'J.I.' base consists of 2 parts, by weight, of hoof and horn, 2 of superphosphate, and 1 of sulphate of potash. When we talk of John Innes No. 1, 2 or 3, we mean that it has 1, 2 or 3 times the quantity of base fertiliser.

If you have more than enough seedlings for the space available, transport only the sturdiest-looking specimens. Keep the others for a few days until the first appear to have settled in, then either compost them, eat, give or throw them away.

If you buy your vegetables as seedlings from a nursery they should be transplanted to their growing stations in the same way as home-raised seedlings. Avoid buying pale, yellowing, dry, wilting or spindly-looking plants, and only go to a reliable supplier who should at least know the name of the variety of vegetable he is selling. The biggest plants may not be the best as they could have become 'pot-bound', having outgrown their pots so that their roots are overcrowded and probably sticking out of the drainage hole at the bottom of the pot.

If you are transplanting from seed trays, divide the compost into squares with a knife, as if you were slicing up a cake, and remove each seedling with a spoon, making sure you take a good clump of compost with it around the roots. Water the compost first to bind it together.

To remove a seedling from a pot, hold the pot upside down with the fingers of one hand on either side of the stem. Tap the rim of the pot against the edge of a table and the plant should slide out with its compost still intact. If it won't budge tap harder. Plastic pots, milk cartons, yoghurt pots and the like can be cut open with a knife. Tins can be opened with an opener at the bottom. Whatever the container, keep the ball of compost in one lump if you can.

Make a hole in the new, already moistened, potting compost with a dibber, trowel or spoon, large enough to take the ball of compost. This is the moment that peat pots and pellets come into their own. You just have to lower the entire thing, seedling and all, into the hole. The roots will push their way through the peat and into the surrounding compost, and the peat will gradually fall apart. It not only makes the operation easier for you but the plant avoids the shock of being transplanted, which is often a setback to its general development, and there is less risk of root damage.

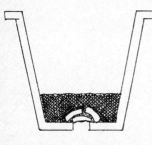

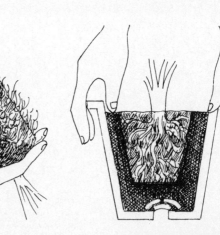

Lower the seedling into the hole up to the level of the first leaves. If you are transplanting to a larger pot or container, as opposed to the open ground, crock the drainage hole in the new pot and put down a layer of compost. Place the seedling and its ball of compost in the middle and fill up the space around it with more compost, pressing it down fairly firmly as you go. The new level of compost should be at the same level as the old. Firm down, water and keep moist. Tomatoes, peppers and other vegetables that need to be supported by stakes should have their canes put in at this stage to avoid the risk of damaging the roots later on. You may have to repot more than once in the lifetime of a plant, if its existing pot becomes too small to hold the expanding root system (i.e. it becomes pot-bound).

If you are transplanting any vegetable to a container that is to stand outdoors, you must prepare it for the culture shock. About a week before transplanting introduce the vegetable to the feeling of a lower temperature and greater ventilation. Transplant on a warm day if possible.

Where growing-space is at a premium, take advantage of techniques such as 'inter-cropping', the sowing of quick-maturing vegetables in the gaps between the slower growers. The former will be ready for harvesting long before the latter will need all their allotted room. And always have another crop ready for sowing or planting just as soon as the previous tenant leaves its container.

Part Three
THE CHOICE OF VEGETABLES

Don't attempt merely to duplicate the vegetables on display at the supermarket or greengrocer. This makes little economic sense; moreover many of them are there not because of their fine tasting qualities, but because they are high-yielding, keep for a long period of time without spoiling, and are bred tough to withstand rough handling and long-distance transportation.

As an indoor farmer concentrate on the valuable crops that are rarely to be seen in the shops, except in wealthy middle-class areas, and then only at exorbitant prices. Choose those whose flavour and vitamin content is vastly superior if gathered minutes instead of days before they reach the cooking pot.

Since most of your cultivating will be in containers, and the amount of space that can be devoted to indoor farming will be limited, pick the varieties of vegetables that take up little room. They can be planted closer together, and need less depth of soil for their roots, but don't necessarily produce a significantly smaller yield than the ordinaries. These mini, baby, stump-rooted, tiny varieties may be hard to come by, except directly from the seed companies, so be sure to send off for their catalogues and order early to avoid disappointment.

Above all you should grow what you like to eat. The selection that follows on pages 109-141 is only a recommended selection, chosen for their suitability for indoor, limited-space and container-cultivation. If you have more room, a garden or allotment, or even a large terrace or access to a flat roof area, there will really be no limit to the range of vegetables that you could grow in a city. A more comprehensive selection could include:

parsnips   cauliflower
onions   Brussels sprouts

Jerusalem artichokes	kale
endive	broccoli
fennel	globe artichokes
celery	turnip
broad beans	dandelion
asparagus	tobacco
kohl-rabi	

And in addition to growing your own food in the confines of a city house or flat take advantage of all the free foods that nature has to offer, just for the picking. Make your Sunday outings into the country a safari for the wild things, as well as a desperate chase after peace and fresh air. Look for, among a host of other edibles:

wild mint
sorrel (for salads and French sorrel soup)
nettles (nettle soup)

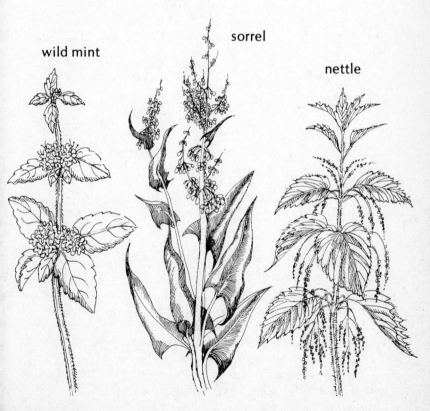

wild mint

sorrel

nettle

elderberry and elderflower

dandelion   mushroom

dandelions (for salads)
mushrooms (be sure to take a good fungi guide
   along, one that clearly indicates the difference
   between the poisonous and edible types)
berries (various kinds)
elderflower (for wine)
all of which abound at the right time of year.

108

AUBERGINE

The aubergine, with its shiny, dark purple fruit, is undoubtedly one of the most handsome of vegetables. Once dismissed by the English as being too exotic it is now rapidly gaining in popularity as a result of holidays in foreign parts, and continental restaurants at home.

Aubergines grow naturally in warm regions but they will successfully flourish indoors provided you can give them plenty of sunshine. They are ideally suited to grow-bag cultivation, where they will gladly cohabit with tomatoes. They will also feel at home in an 8 inch flower pot.

Germinate the seeds at 65 degrees fahrenheit; they will take several days. Sow two, ½ inch deep in a 3 inch peat pot and thin to one seedling leaving the strongest-looking specimen in each pot. Move to a grow-bag, or 'pot on', when the seedling is 3 to 4 inches high. Or you can sow the seeds directly in the grow-bag, thinning out to leave four plants per bag.

Provide support for the aubergine to grow on. Pinch out the main shoot when the plant reaches a height of about 9 inches, and later restrict each plant to a maximum of four fruits by removing excess flowers and stopping the growth of the laterals, or side shoots.

You must assist pollination by a daily tapping of the stems after the flowers have formed, or dust the flowers with a camel-hair brush or feather. A daily syringe will also help pollination and prevent red spider mite. Give the aubergine an occasional feed of liquid fertiliser, about every ten days once the flowers have set, and water well and regularly. Harvest the fruits while their coats are still glossy or else they will begin to taste bitter. Cut them off the plant with secateurs or a sharp knife.

Varieties: Short Tom, Burpee Hybrid.

The simplest way to cook aubergine is to slice, coat with flour, and fry until golden. To prevent their tasting bitter you should first sprinkle salt over the slices and leave them to drain in a colander for half an hour. Wash the slices in cold water and dry before flouring and frying. Aubergine can also be baked in tomato sauce, with mozzarella and parmesan cheese, or part boiled, scooped out, stuffed with whatever you fancy, and baked.

BEANS, DWARF FRENCH

The best bean choice for the indoor farmer. They are very high yielding for the space they occupy, and are easily grown in pots or boxes in a sunny spot.

The seeds require a minimum germination temperature of 60 degrees fahrenheit. Sow 8 seeds in an 8 inch pot, or 12 to a 12 inch, 2 inches deep, and thin to half that number. The thinnings, if they appear strong, could be transplanted to their own pot or box rather than wasted. Put sticks into the pots at this stage for future staking to avoid the risk of damaging the roots later on (although staking is really optional).

Syringe the beans daily to help the flowers set and prevent red spider mite. Feed every ten days with liquid fertiliser once the pods appear. Keep them

well ventilated, but out of draughts, and you
shouldn't have any problems. Harvest early, while
the pods are 3 to 4 inches long and at their
tenderest. Snap them off the plant and more will
follow.

If your home has an outside growing area, try a
few climbing beans, French or runners, up a trellis to
hide an otherwise boring wall or unsightly drainpipe.

Varieties: Tendergreen, The Prince, Masterpiece. For
a small climber try Hammond's Dwarf Scarlet
Runner.

If you gather them young all French beans can be
cooked whole, after a mere topping and tailing.
Steam or boil in a little water for a few minutes.
They can also be cooled under the cold water tap,
drained and fried fast in butter and garlic. Nice cold
too. When served whole they are usually referred to
as *haricots verts;* alternatively they can be shelled
and eaten as *flageolets,* but the waste or the shell
makes that rather extravagant for the indoor farmer.

BEETROOT

Both the top greens and the beautiful red roots of the beetroot can be eaten, so making it an excellent value-for-space crop. They are well-suited to window-box cultivation, preferably on an outside ledge since they prefer a cool temperature. They will also tolerate partial shade.

Sow the seeds singly, 1 inch deep, after an overnight soaking in water. Each beetroot seed in fact comprises more than one true seed. Any excess growth can later be thinned to leave one main plant, kept 4 inches from its neighbour. Use such thinnings, which cannot be transplanted, for greens since their food value is high.

Regular watering is essential. Harvest beetroot while they are about the size of a golf ball. Twist the foliage off the top as cutting will make the beetroot bleed and you might feel guilty.

Varieties: Boltardy, Detroit, Burpee Golden, Little Ball.

You can enjoy beetroot both hot or cold, but remember to boil them first in salted water for about half an hour. Then peel and serve. You can also bake beets. Cook — boil, steam or stir fry — and consume the leafy tops just like spinach, or enjoy them cold in a salad.

CABBAGE

Most cabbages have to be ruled out of consideration from the indoor farmer's repertoire on account of their size, but one or two of the baby-headed varieties would certainly be worth a try, especially as commercially-raised cabbages tend to be excessively dosed with insecticides.

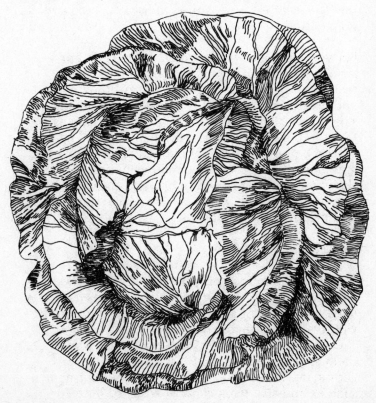

Sow the seeds ½ inch deep in seed trays. Prick out when they have grown their first true leaves, and later transplant to their final growing positions, a window box or an 8 inch pot perhaps, when they have grown five or six leaves. Firm them down well. Feed with liquid fertiliser and water well whenever they appear dry. Harvest when the heads are still hard and solid.

Varieties: Baby Head. Or try quick maturing (about 8 weeks from seed to maturity) Chinese cabbage, Sampan or Pe Tsai, which should be sown ¼ inch deep in its final growing position, which can be partially shady. (Sow 4 inches apart and thin to 8 inches. Water well and tie the leaves together when it begins to heart.) Chinese cabbage has a milder flavour than other cabbage and can be used as a substitute for lettuce in salads. If you take just a few leaves at a time it will carry on cropping over a long period.

For years cabbage has suffered a bad reputation since, more than any other vegetable, its taste, texture and goodness is easily destroyed by over-enthusiastic boilers. Boil it in just a tiny amount of salted water or chicken stock for just as long as it takes to become tender. Thoroughly drain, and season before serving. Or shred cabbage across the grain and stir fry for a few minutes in hot oil, flavoured with garlic and onion, and then add a touch of soy sauce. And you don't have to be a rabbit to relish raw cabbage.

CARROT

The small, stump-rooted varieties of carrot should be chosen for home cultivation in containers as they need less depth of soil. Its foliage, fine and fern like, will rival that of many house plants.

Carrot seed should be sown where you want them to grow, and will take quite a while to germinate. Sow thinly in a cool part of your home, such as an east-facing window ledge or in the

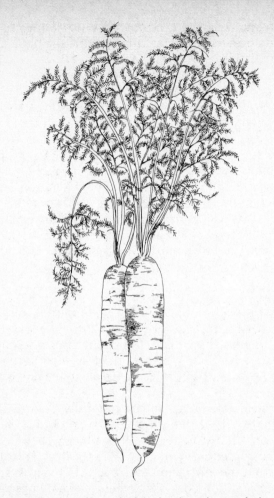

bedroom which will probably be less heated than
the other rooms. Their minimum germination
temperature is 40 degrees fahrenheit. As carrot seeds
are so tiny mix them with some sand or peat to
ensure an even spread, and cover with a fine layer
of potting compost.

Carrots grow best in a light, sandy soil which
should never contain manure, fresh compost or
stones as the roots may grow misshapen. Thin the
seedlings as they begin to crowd each other out —
later thinnings can be eaten as a delicacy. Aim to
end up with individual carrots growing 3 inches
apart, or grow them about a dozen in a 12 inch pot.

Pull them up before the tops begin to yellow — try an odd one every so often till they look the right size for harvesting.

Varieties: Early Nantes, Little Finger, Short 'n Sweet, or any other of the stump- or round-rooted carrots recommended for growing in shallow soils.

Pick them young and you will have only to scrub and steam them for a few minutes, instead of peeling and boiling at great cost to their flavour and vitamin content. Serve with butter and some of your herbs. Grate raw carrots to brighten up any salad, and don't forget that carrots can form the basic ingredients of cakes, tarts, wine and even jams.

CELERIAC

Celery proper would be rather an ambitious vegetable for the indoor farmer, but those who enjoy its refreshing taste and crispy texture could try celeriac, which some people think is even better. It is grown for its root, as opposed to the stalks of celery.

Because celeriac seeds are painfully slow to germinate, speed things up by first sprouting the seeds on a moist paper towel or blotting paper, at 65 to 70 degrees fahrenheit, and in the dark. Transfer those that develop 'radicals', the initial root system, each to a 3 inch peat pot. When the seedlings have developed their first true leaves, transplant the peat pots to their final home. Celeriac will grow best in a 10 inch pot or similar sized box or other container. Water regularly and feed now and then with liquid fertiliser. Add a little more compost round the roots as they swell to keep them white, and cut off any side shoots that appear. Harvest celeriac when they are fist size by pulling from the pot.

Varieties: Globus, Marble Ball.

Cut off the top and scrub or scrape the root thoroughly. Cut into slices, keeping them in lemon

116

(acidulated) water to prevent browning. Dip in salt
and eat, or grate into a salad. Or turn it into
celeriac remoulade by mixing grated bits with
mustard powder and mayonnaise. Or cut into cubes,
boil for about 15 minutes, and serve with butter,
chives and parsley, or with an onion or cheese
sauce. Or add celeriac to stews for finer flavouring.
Or braise it. Or steam it. Or throw it at your worst
enemy.

COURGETTE

Courgettes are the small and succulent relatives of the marrow. The vegetable's flowers and foliage will look as magnificent as those of the most exotic house plants, but they do take up quite a bit of space when fully grown. Grow the bush, rather than the trailing, varieties in a large, deep container, keep it on a balcony or patio, and if you mount the container on castors you will be able to wheel it round to follow the sun, and bring it indoors on chilly evenings. Courgettes can also grow from deep, hanging baskets in a sunny window and they will cascade down the side.

Soak the seeds overnight before sowing two to each 3 inch peat pot. Stand them on their edge, ½ inch deep, and germinate at 65 degrees fahrenheit. Thin to one per pot and transplant two or three peat

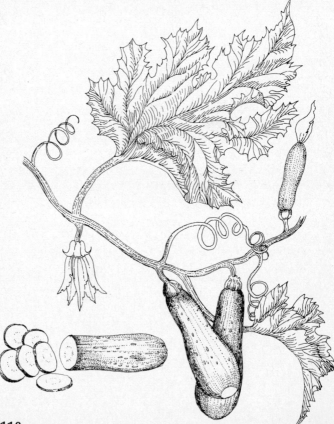

pots to each large tub or box filled with potting compost. It is a good idea to enrich the compost beforehand with dried manure, and to sink a small flower pot in the centre of the box so that water poured into the pot will go straight to the roots and miss the leaves and stalks. This will lessen the risks of stem rot.

Courgettes like plenty of sun and ideally prefer a daytime temperature of 70 and a night of 65 degrees farenheit. Be careful not to overwater, and feed every week with liquid manure once the fruits start to swell. But before that stage is reached you must pollinate the female flowers, recognisable by the bump, the swelling courgette-to-be, behind the petals. Remove the petals from a male flower and invert it onto the female. Use a different male flower each time. When the fruits reach between 4 and 6 inches long they will be ready for harvesting. Don't allow them to grow any bigger. The more you pick, the more you'll get.

Varieties: Zucchini, Aristocrat, Golden.

You can eat the stalks, flowers, leaves as well as the fruit of the courgette. They all join forces in making real minestrone. Otherwise cook the courgettes whole, after topping and tailing, in as little water as possible. Drain, while they still remain firm to the touch, add butter, and cook for a few more minutes. You can also slice and fry in flour or fritter in batter. They are superb served cold with a vinaigrette dressing or in yoghurt. Or simmer slowly in butter and crushed garlic for up to an hour (with the lid on). Add fresh parsley and they taste every bit as good as *escargots,* with none of the disadvantages.

CUCUMBER

Since the average family consumes so few during the course of the year it hardly seems worth giving up the space to grow them. They are not particularly nutritious, taste no better when enjoyed straight from the vine, and are quite difficult to grow. However, if you are keen to have a go . . .

Ridge cucumbers will be the easiest but should be raised outside, on a balcony or terrace, in a sunny and sheltered spot. They will grow well from large pots especially the Japanese varieties which can be trained up a wall or trellis screen, and so take up little room. Germinate the seeds indoors in a temperature of at least 60 degrees fahrenheit, sowing two seeds blunt end downwards, ½ inch deep, in a 3 inch peat pot. Thin to leave the strongest, transplant to a large 12 inch pot or similar container, and move outside in mid-spring when the weather is warm, and after the third or fourth true leaves appear.

The indoor, or 'frame', cucumbers are raised from seed in the same way as the outdoor (ridge) type but at a slightly higher temperature (65 to 70 degrees fahrenheit). They will grow best in warm, centrally heated, splendour, 70 degrees fahrenheit plus, and in a Turkish bath atmosphere that most other vegetables, including tomatoes, cannot stand. Try them in the bathroom if it is light enough, but bear in mind that cucumbers like ventilation as well as humidity. A window greenhouse that can be sealed off from the room is the perfect place to grow, or indulge, them.

Apart from the varieties that can be raised without any support, train the main stem of the cucumber upwards and pinch off the growing tip when it is as high as you want it to grow (or after half a dozen leaves have formed, to encourage the growth of side shoots). Train the side branches along wires, 6-8 inches apart, so that they grow horizontally from the main stem, and limit the number of fruits to two for every side-shoot by pinching out their growing tips after the second leaf. Or try growing them from hanging baskets, especially the smaller pickling cucumbers.

Syringe two or three times a day to keep their atmosphere humid and keep red spider mite, cucumber enemy-number-one, at bay. Keep the compost moist, but avoid letting water reach the

stalks for the same reasons as for courgettes. Be careful not to overwater as immature fruits may rot or drop. Feed with liquid fertiliser at fortnightly intervals when the cukes begin to swell.

Ridge cucumbers have to be pollinated if the fruits are to develop but if they are grown where the bees will see to it naturally, you won't have to bother. Indoor 'frame' cucumbers should not be pollinated as it makes the cucumbers grow club shaped and taste bitter. Either remove the male flowers as they appear (the ones without the swelling behind) or grow an all-female variety. Don't leave the fruits on the plants too long as this can also make them taste bitter.

Varieties: *Outdoor:* Patio Pik, Midget, or the Japanese small varieties (grow three plants to each 12 inch pot — they will take up little room).

Indoor: Conqueror (it can stand a less humid atmosphere than most others and so will grow side by side with tomatoes). Improved Telegraph (neither are all-female); however Rocket and Femspot are.

Although the cucumber tends only to make its appearance in summer salads, in the company of tomatoes, lettuce, spring onions and apple, it is really more versatile than that. Slices can be flour-coated, fried and served in a hollandaise sauce. Or steam larger chunks for a very short time and serve with butter and herbs. Or try stuffing them, first removing all the seeds, and then baking.

LEEKS

Leeks are the mild-flavoured members of the onion family as well as being the Welsh national emblem. Grow a row or two on a winter window sill.

It is easier to buy ready-raised seedlings from a nursery and make 6 inch holes for them to be dropped into than to grow from seed. They will grow in any compost-filled container with a minimum depth of 9 inches, even in the larger-sized coffee tins. Plant them 6 inches apart in a window box. If you grow leeks from seed start them off in the spring for winter harvesting as they will take a long time, about 140 days from seed to maturity.

The seedlings should be dropped into holes leaving just the tips of the leaves poking above the level of the compost. Fill up the holes with water, not compost. Water well and regularly, and occasionally feed. Harvest while they are still quite small as they will taste better than when king-sized.

Varieties: Musselburgh, Marble Pillar.

Boil, poach, bake or braise your leeks, perhaps served au gratin, or make a leek pie. But first prepare by thoroughly washing to remove any traces of compost or grains of sand lodged between the

leaves, and trim off the tops leaving about 2 inches of green. The rest can be used for stock or flavouring soups and stews.

LETTUCE

A crop that no indoor farmer can overlook. They can be grown throughout the year and offer enormous returns for the spaces they occupy. Grow them here, there and everywhere, even slipping them into your pots or grow-bags as soon as other vegetables have been harvested. Their taste will be vastly superior to shop-bought versions.

Sow a few seeds, every two weeks to ensure a continuous supply, thinly to a depth of ¼ inch and germinate at 60 degrees fahrenheit. Some growers advise a temperature of 50 degrees for the first 3 days (as the seeds may remain dormant if the temperature is too high), but that may be impractical. Thin as they grow to 6 inches apart, and eat these baby leaves; if you sow pelleted seeds you will, of course, be sowing at the correct distance in the first place. Lettuces will also grow individually and most attractively in 4 or 5 inch pots. Get in a few radishes at the same time as sowing the lettuces since they will be ready for harvesting before the lettuce leaves take over.

Water well so that the lettuces keep on coming quickly and crisply, and keep all indoor ones well-ventilated. They will perform best where they get plenty of light but where the temperature remains on the cool side, the optimum being 55 degrees day, 48 night.

Harvest by pulling up the whole plant when it has

formed a firm heart, and remove the roots and the lower leaves with a knife. Do not expect your indoor lettuces to be the perfect-headed sort that commercial growers turn out because you will probably have less available light. Be content with plenty of fine-tasting leaves. If you harvest while they are small you could treat each person to their own individual lettuce on a plate.

Varieties: For outdoor growing choose the variety that is suitable for growing at the particular time of the year, since the winter sort will 'bolt', or run to seed, if the temperature is too warm, and summer lettuces won't grow at all during cold, short days. These considerations will also apply to varieties chosen in relation to the normal temperature indoors; winter varieties may not fare well in a centrally heated home in the middle of winter. Tom Thumb is the crispy, tennis-ball sized lettuce that is best suited to growing in small containers. Otherwise choose the cabbage, or leafy, lettuces, and some of the Cos varieties, such as Little Gem, Parris Cos or Lobjoits Green Cos (a leafy lettuce that will produce twice the amount in half the time it takes many other varieties). You might also like to try Lambs Lettuce — also known as corn salad — or the peppery-flavoured Roquette.

Always tear lettuce by hand — the edges of cut leaves turn brown. Wash and dry completely before dressing. Try a pure green salad rather than always throwing in a tomato or two to 'brighten' it up. And give lettuce soup a try.

PEAS

Although peas offer rather a low yield in relation to the space they occupy, their milky sweet taste when freshly picked and cooked certainly justifies a couple of pots full. Their nutritional value also falls off considerably with delays between picking and cooking, so shop-bought peas can never be as good as your own.

Sow six seeds, 1½ inches deep, in a twelve inch pot. Firm down well. The dwarf varieties will not need supporting, but a twiggy branch stuck in the middle of the pot, or twine tied round four canes pushed into the compost, will induce a bigger crop.

Peas like a well-ventilated, fairly dry atmosphere, with a daytime high in the mid-sixties and a night-time temperature around 55 degrees. Pick when small and sweet, from the bottom upwards.

Varieties: Choose the dwarfs, such as Mighty Midget or Little Marvel. They produce plenty of pods for their stature. Mangetout, or Sugar Pea, varieties grow taller, and can be eaten pod and all after topping and tailing. The Asparagus Pea is hard to come by: it tastes of asparagus.

Cook whole. Ordinary peas should be boiled or steamed till just tender and served with a blob of butter. Keep the pods for stock or as a base for pea soup.

PEPPERS, SWEET

Although better-known on the continent, their good looks, versatility in the kitchen, high vitamin content and enormous shop price, make them a must for the indoor farmer.

It is vital that peppers get plenty of sun. They should be grown either in a south facing window or on a sunny balcony, perhaps in a grow-bag. Germinate the seeds at 65 degrees fahrenheit in 3 inch peat pots, ½ inch deep (or sow in seed trays and prick out to the peat pots). Later transplant them to 8 inch pots or the grow-bag. They will need supporting, so put the canes in when you transplant.

When the flowers appear hand-pollinate them

with a camel-hair brush to encourage the fruits to set. As soon as you see the first signs of fruiting, when the plant is 6 to 8 inches high, pinch out the growing tip. Syringe daily with a fine mist spray to provide humidity, assist pollination and prevent red spider mite. Restrict the number of fruits per plant to six or seven. Keep peppers warm, water well and feed with liquid manure when the fruits start to swell. Pick while green or leave until they turn to red, although their taste won't change that much with the colour. You could get up to 30 fruits per plant.

Varieties: New Ace, Canapé. You could also grow the hot peppers — chili, cayenne — in the same way.

The white pith inside the pepper must be removed when you prepare them in the kitchen or else they will taste bitter. Eaten raw, the pepper's clean flavour goes well with most salads. Peppers can also be fried in oil, with onions, or added to stews and curries. For stuffing and baking you should cut out a plug from the stem end, remove the pith, stuff with, say, rice, meat and tomatoes, and replace the plug before cooking.

POTATOES

No doubt a rather surprising choice for the indoor farm. Certainly maincrop potatoes are out of the question, but one or two pots of early 'spring' spuds would be a real treat for a tired palate. And they contain more protein, and are less fattening, than you suspect.

Buy seed potatoes, certified as being disease free, from a reliable supplier. Stand them upright, eyes or 'rose end' uppermost, in egg trays and place in a cool and not too bright area of your home to sprout, a process known as 'chitting'. Rub off all but three or four strong looking sprouts on the upper part of the potato. If the seed potato is a large one you could cut it into smaller pieces, each one with its own strong sprout.

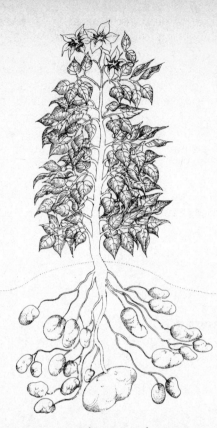

Half fill a 10 or 12 inch pot with compost, place a seed potato in the middle, shoots uppermost, and cover with an inch or two of compost. Add more compost or peat as the foliage, or haulm, grows upwards, firming down gently as you do. This will encourage the formation of tubers, the future potatoes, beneath the surface. When the compost reaches the top of the pot cover the pot with black polythene to keep the light off the compost and cut a hole in the middle for the haulm to grow through.

Potatoes will grow best in a low temperature with plenty of fresh air. Feed occasionally with a fertiliser. Lift the lot out before the haulm begins to yellow.

Varieties: There are nearly a hundred different varieties grown in Britain, but relatively few are ever available for the amateur market. For an early batch try Epicure, Arran Pilot or Duke of York.

After a quick scrub, new potatoes are best gently boiled, or steamed, and eaten in their jackets with butter and parsley, and perhaps a hint of mint. As an added bonus for the indoor farmer, aim to have some ready for harvesting and enjoying with your Christmas dinner. Potato salad can be made with boiled but still firm potatoes chopped up with chives, parsley, hard boiled eggs, a little garlic and mayonnaise. Add a splash of lemon juice to their cooking water to prevent new potatoes from discolouring.

RADISHES

A super-fast grower, taking less than thirty days to move from seed to fully fledged radish. And they will fit into any odd space as catch crops or intercrops round slower growers. They don't mind the

shade and so will grow in their own pots or boxes in duller north- or east-facing windows.

Sprinkle the seeds thinly, cover with a little compost, and firm down. Try to sow a few every couple of weeks to keep a steady supply coming, or sow a new seedling every time you pull out a radish. Thin the seeds to 3 inches apart, or even squeeze together a wee bit closer, as the seedlings grow. Keep well watered and cool—they will grow best at 55 degrees.

Varieties: French Breakfast, Cherry Belle.

Radishes are catabolic, demanding more calories to digest than they add to your body, so they are a useful food for weight-conscious eaters. Although radishes are usually consumed raw, traditionally in salads, they can also be cooked. Boil whole for ten minutes with or without their foliage and serve with butter and sea salt, or mash, bake or fry. Add them to soup or stews.

SALSIFY

Salsify is a vegetable rarely seen in the shops, and well worth growing for that very reason. The taste is rather special and somewhat oystery. Scorzonera is similar to salsify except that its roots are black-skinned.

Salsify can be grown in a 10 or 12 inch flower pot, or similar size or preferably even deeper, container, but bear in mind that they will have to stay there several months before you can eat them. Sow the seeds ½ inch deep in pairs, four pairs to each 10 inch pot. Thin to leave the strongest-looking seedlings. Or grow 6 inches apart in a trough-shaped container. Keep moist and you will have little else to do or worry about. Harvest carefully as these roots are quite delicate.

Varieties: Sandwich Island, Mammoth.

When cooking salsify or scorzonera you should first

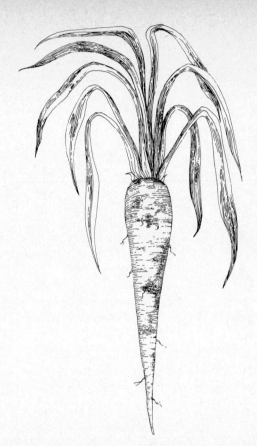

scald and scrape the roots rather than try to peel
them. Peeling is both a difficult task and will release
too much of their flavour and goodness in the
cooking pot. Alternatively scrape salsify after it has
been cooked. Simmer in salted water and a little
lemon juice until they are tender (about 20-30
minutes). Serve with a cream sauce, or sauté in
butter.

SPINACH

Spinach takes up less room than you might imagine.
It is quick in producing its luxuriant green foliage
which helps to build up Popeye muscles. But
spinach will not fare well in a hot, dry atmosphere
as it will probably run to seed.

Perpetual spinach, or spinach beet, although never classed as true spinach by an expert horticulturist, is nevertheless the best choice for you. The leaves should be picked young, before their flavour gets too strong, and continuously, so that more will take their place. You can, in fact, cut up to half the outer leaves at any one time without causing a set-back to its growth. Just one or two plants could therefore last you, more or less, throughout the year. And it is unlikely to run to seed, especially if positioned on a north or east facing window sill.

Sow the seeds 1 inch deep and thin to 3 inches. A few weeks later, as the seedlings begin to crowd each other, thin again, taking alternative plants and leaving those remaining 6 inches apart. These thinnings can be eaten. Or you can grow one spinach in a 4 or 5 inch pot.

Varieties: Perpetual Spinach. Try New Zealand spinach if you live in an overheated and sun-bathed apartment; it can stand quite a high temperature but does take up quite a bit more room. It is also a cut-and-come-again vegetable, so keep those picking fingers busy to encourage the arrival of green recruits.

Steam spinach till it begins to wilt, but give it a thorough wash first. You can cook spinach without adding any water to the pan. The water present in the leaves will be sufficient if you put them in a tightly covered pan and cook for a few minutes. Serve spinach with lemon. Try frying it or eating raw like lettuce. The young and tender stalks of perpetual spinach can be cooked and served like asparagus.

SPRING ONIONS

Where space is at a premium you will be better off just growing green, or spring, onions rather than their bigger brothers. They can be intercropped with other salads in a window box, or grown in a pot indoors. Whatever way, there are unlikely to be problems.

Sow the seeds ½ inch deep in clusters or rows, and at intervals of two or three weeks to provide a steady stream for your salads. Thin to 2 inches apart and put the thinnings in your stock pot. You can actually grow at least a dozen in a 10 inch pot if you're not hung up over their individual size. Spring onions will grow best in a daytime temperature of 60 degrees fahrenheit, and 55 at night, but are fairly flexible in their demands. Keep their compost moist and try to give them as sunny and open a spot as you can afford.

Varieties: White Lisbon, a standard favourite and a quick cropper with a mild flavour. You could also have a try at growing pickling onions, the mild but almost impossible to get hold of potato onion, or the tree onion whose bulbs first appear at the end

of the stems in place of flowers. If you insist on
devoting somewhere to ordinary onions, plant 'sets',
or small bulbs, rather than trying to raise them from
seed, or grow milder tasting shallot sets.

Spring onions can be added to stews, or pierced on
a kebab skewer, but are usually eaten raw.

SWISS CHARD

The leaves of Swiss chard (also known as seakale beet or leafy beet) are finer tasting than spinach and the stalks can be cooked and even passed off as a poor man's asparagus. In other words the vegetable is a good two-in-one choice for the grower with limited space. It is also incredibly easy to grow and will do even better than lettuce in hot, dry conditions. In further praise, Swiss chard is high yielding, won't object to being stuck in partial shade, and can seldom be seen in the shops because it deteriorates rapidly in transit. It also looks good, so what are you waiting for . . .

Grow it from seed, sown ½ inch deep. Thin to 9

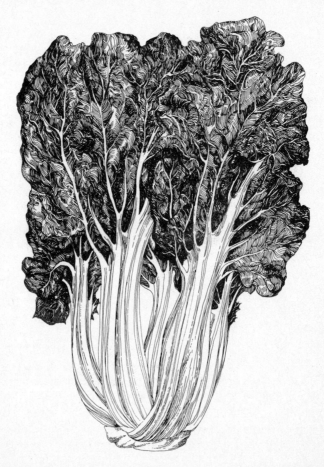

inches apart (if sown in open ground as opposed to individual pots) and eat the thinnings as greens. Water liberally and feed occasionally. Harvest a few leaves, by pulling out their stems, and new ones will replace them.

Varieties: known just as Swiss chard or seakale beet.

The smaller leaves can be eaten raw in salads, and the bigger ones are best steamed like spinach till they begin to wilt, or gently simmered in a stock. Serve with melted butter or a cheese or Hollandaise sauce. Alternatively boil or steam the leaf stalks like asparagus.

TOMATOES

Love apples, as tomatoes were once called, have a history shrouded in myth and superstition. Originating in Peru, tomatoes came to the United States where they were regarded as having both aphrodisiac and poisonous qualities. Their reputation was changed by one Colonel Johnson when he courageously ate an entire basket of these 'wolf peaches', in front of an expectant crowd, on the steps of the court house in Salem, New Jersey. Several people fainted in horror. Today tomatoes are the most popular of all the home-grown crops, and should certainly form the staple one for an indoor farmer. They are an excellent source of vitamins A, B and C.

Sow two seeds ½ inch deep in 3 inch peat pots or sow thinly in seed trays and later prick out to the peat pots when their first true leaves appear. Germinate at a minimum and constant temperature of 70 degrees fahrenheit. If both the seeds in the peat pot germinate, take out the weaker-looking one. Artificial light is a great boon to the seedling's early days, kept on for 16 hours a day for the first 3 weeks of their lives.

Once the true leaves have become fairly well established, pot on to 4 or 5 inch pots, always handling by the leaves to prevent damaging their

delicate stems. When the seedlings are about 8
inches high, looking sturdy and rich green in colour
and just after the first flower truss has appeared,
transplant the tomatoes to their final growing
position. That may be a 10 or 12 inch pot, a window
box, and inside sill container, or a grow-bag. Do not
put them outside until all risk of frost has passed;
tomatoes will grow to perfection in a daytime
temperature of 70 degrees, and a night-time of 60.
Indoor atmospheres must be kept well ventilated.

In their natural state tomatoes would grow lying
down, so stake them when they are finally
transplanted, tying the stems loosely to a cane

support with soft string or raffia, re-tying them as they grow, or alternatively, you can loop the string round the base of the stem and attach it to an overhead supporting wire. Carefully twist the plant around the string as it grows. Some dwarf or trailing varieties can be grown in pots or hanging baskets and just left to trail over the side.

With most tomatoes (the pixie varieties being an exception) you should continually pinch out the side shoots that grow from the leaf axils, the angle between the main stem and a leaf stalk, using your finger and thumb. This will concentrate the plant's

energy into a single main stem. Pinch out the main stem after five or six 'trusses' or flowerheads have developed outdoors, or eight or ten indoors at two leaves above a developing truss. This will encourage the production of fruit rather than foliage.

Tap the branches daily while they are in bloom to facilitate pollination, and syringe with tepid water. Feed well and on a regular basis, with tomato fertiliser (which contains a high proportion of potash) once the flowers have formed. Follow the instructions on the label on the amount and frequency required. Water sparingly until the fruit begins to set, and then always at regular intervals.

The plant must be kept moist; never alternate between drought and flood. Tie the leaves back to enable the fruit to get plenty of light, and once the fruit begins to colour you can gradually cut away the lower leaves, working your way up the plant; don't over-prune as the leaves are still functioning as the plant's food factories.

Harvest your tomatoes as they colour by picking individuals or cutting off the whole ripened truss from the main stem with scissors or secateurs. Never try to pull a tomato away from the calyx (the cap). Ripen any still green in a warm, dark place, and not in a sunny window as is usually done, and use the green ones for chutney, jams or pickles. The earlier you can begin to pick, the more fruit you will get. After harvesting burn or throw the plant away.

Varieties: Pixie, Tiny Tim. These are the small bush varieties that are well suited to indoor cultivation since they take up much less room than the conventional tomato plants, and will require less looking after. They are fast to ripen, produce a good yield for their size, and will flourish entirely under artificial light. Cherry tomatoes can be grown from hanging baskets and will make a fine display if interplanted with chives or parsley. Otherwise, if you don't mind masses of greenery in front of your living room window you could grow more or less any variety you like.

Eat tomatoes raw, stewed, fried or baked. If you want to peel them before using them in a dish, or to perhaps make a genuine Italian sauce for pasta, scald in boiling water and the skin will come away easily. Larger tomatoes, if you can find room to grow them indoors, can be stuffed with almost anything. And try making some real tomato soup that will make you wonder what happened to the tomatoes in the tinned stuff.

If you fancy trying your hand at experimental horticulture you could try raising a 'Tompot', a vegetable with a tomato top and a potato root. Both belong to the Solaneceae (nightshade) family.

Sprout a potato in the normal way and remove all but the strongest looking shoot. Plant 1 inch below the surface in a 5 inch pot of compost. After about three weeks select a tomato seedling with a stem of similar thickness to the potato shoot. Cut off the top of the tomato to leave 3 inches or 4 inches of stem, and shorten the potato shoot to leave a 2 inch to 3 inch stump. Carefully cut a 'Λ' shaped notch in the potato stem, using a clean razor blade, and an inverted 'V', or a 'Λ' in the base of the tomato stem so that they will make a perfect fit.

Make sure that air doesn't get trapped within the graft, and seal with special grafting tape of raffia, tying it to a stake to hold it firm. After about three weeks the two should be united. You can help by enclosing the plant in a plastic bag, which is held off the leaves by bamboo canes until the graft area begins to swell. Then grow, and feed, like an ordinary tomato. Both 'fruits' should be ready at about the same time.

Part Four

VEGETABLE ENEMIES

WEEDS

If you use sterilised potting compost for your indoor, balcony or patio crops it is highly unlikely that you will ever be troubled by weeds. If they do appear they will rob your vegetables of water, nutrients, space and light as well as help spread pests and diseases; so get rid of them. If the compost is well moistened you will be able to pull them out quite easily, prising them up with a fork or a small hand-weeder. Pull them out whole — if you break them off by the stem it will only stimulate their growth. Be careful not to disturb the vegetables.

The guide that follows covers pests and diseases that could occur in both indoor cultivated vegetables and those raised in a garden. Don't let its length put you off since an indoor farmer would be very unlucky to come across more than two or three of these ailments in an entire growing season.

PESTS

Vegetables grown indoors are far less likely to be attacked by pests than those raised outdoors, especially if you live high up out of pest flying-range. The risks are also reduced when crops are grown on a small scale.

The actual bandits that maraud vegetables are few relative to the vast number of good insects that offer immense assistance to the grower. The great mistake in using all-purpose insecticides is that they tend to kill these allies, such as those that feed on the baddies (like ladybirds), pollinate (such as bees), aerate the soil (like earthworms), and so on. Pesticides harm other forms of wild life, too, and can be damaging to your own health, especially considering how they are made increasingly more potent to compensate for the developing immunity of the pests.

There is, however, no such thing as a 'safe' pesticide — it wouldn't be able to do its job if it were absolutely safe. Those of vegetative origin, like derris, malathion and pyrethrum, are less harmful and non-persistent — their killing power will last only a limited time and certainly will have gone by the time you eat the vegetables. But even before using these sprays try to pick off the insects with your fingers or tweezers. Some can be rubbed off with a matchstick with cotton wool on the end soaked in methylated spirits. Their eggs and grubs can usually be washed off with a hard jet of water or a spray. Keep a constant look out for the insects, their grubs and the eggs, often found on the undersides of leaves, and signs of their presence, like tiny bites out of leaves and stems, or the plants' loss of colour and wilting appearance. If seedlings and leafy vegetables are growing outside in a window box or balcony, protect by some sort of netting against birds.

And the larger your growing space, the wiser it would be to study 'companion planting' techniques, using certain plants' aromatic qualities to keep the pests away.

Aphids (greenfly, blackfly)
May attack brassicas, carrot, beans, tomato, swiss chard, lettuce, courgette, peas, cucumber, marrow, peppers, spinach. Aphids suck juices from the plant thereby causing direct damage and help to spread virus disease. They may be repelled by the scent of onions, chives or garlic growing nearby. Hose off with a strong jet of water. Or use a derris/pyrethrum mix. Both the latter substances are toxic, otherwise they wouldn't be able to get rid of the aphids, but they are safe for humans and pets with the exception of fish. They are not persistent, but use them in the evening outdoors after the bees have returned to their hives, and when the air is still so that the spray goes on the plants and not up the road or on you.

Red Spider Mite
May strike beans, aubergine, tomato, cucumber and peppers, leaving a trail of mottled leaves in hot, dry weather. Increase humidity with a fine mist sprayer or use derris/pyrethrum.

Asparagus beetle
Their grubs can be got rid of with derris nicotine or Gamma BHC (Lindane). The asparagus beetle has a black and red body with black and yellow wing cases. If you should ever see the orange- and black-striped Colorado beetle in the vicinity of your potatoes, report it to a policeman. Other types of beetle could trouble cucumber and beans — use pyrethrum.

Gall Weevil
Enemy of the brassica family, and sometimes turnips. The Pea Weevil can get to peas, and the rare Bean Weevil to beans. They appear in dry, warm weather and nibble away at leaf edges, but can be deterred by dusting the soil when planting with derris or Gamma BHC (Lindane) but this is a persistent chemical which will kill some of the helpful insects. Infected plants should be burnt.

Earwigs
They eat the leaves of several vegetables, particularly lettuce. Kill them when you see them or use a proprietary bait.

Eelworm (nematodes)
The larvae of these invisible pests get into the roots of potatoes, onions, beets and sometimes strawberries, peas and tomatoes may be their victims. Proper rotation and a fertile soil is the best prevention, derris the best cure. Burn any infected crops.

Slugs and snails
They enjoy a wide range of crops. A cinder or soot path round the vegetables acts as a barrier, or trap them by sinking an aluminium pie dish into the

ground at soil level and fill with milk or beer; slugs
are particularly attracted to it, fall in and drown.
You can also buy methiocarb (or metaldehyde)
pellets, but cover them with a tile or an old plate
so that pets or birds won't eat them.

Carrot fly
Its maggots eat the roots of carrots (celery, parsley,
celeriac and parsnips sometimes). You can buy pre-
treated seeds. Be careful when thinning not to leave
any bits lying around, and firm, the soil well
afterwards. Sow onions (or sage) in the next row to
jam the scent signal of the carrots. Sprinkle wood
ash around. In the last resort use Gamma BHC
(Lindane).

Cabbage butterfly and moth
The caterpillars eat the leaves of brassicas. Look
underneath for signs of the eggs. Never leave bits of
leaf around. Repelled by sage, mint and rosemary.
Destroy by picking off by hand, or use derris.

Cabbage root fly
Lays eggs near cabbages (also radishes, turnips and
swedes) and the grubs eat the roots and stems of the
plant below soil level. A sprinkling of wood ash
around will help to prevent this happening as the
flies won't lay their eggs on it. As a further
precaution you could plant the cabbage seedling
through a hole made in a disc of rubber underfelt.
Seal the slit from the edge of the disc to the centre
hole with sticky tape. Or water every 2 weeks with a
teaspoon of Jeyes fluid in a gallon of water. After
the event use pyrethrum or gamma BHC (Lindane).

White fly
Brassicas (especially cabbage), tomatoes and
cucumbers are all vulnerable. Syringe the leaves
with a mixture of ¼ lb of pure soap to one gallon
of water, or the undersides with nicotine *only* if the
vegetables are at least two weeks off from the
eating stage. Or try derris or pyrethrum.

Leather jackets

The larvae of Daddy Long Legs feed on the stems
and roots of plants below the surface, as well as
coming above ground at night to eat the leaves.
Entice them out in the daytime with bran and the
birds will probably get them.

Millipedes

Not to be confused with the friendly centipede; the
millipede moves slower, has 2 pairs of legs to each
body segment, curls up when disturbed, and should
be exterminated before it gets to your lettuce and
some root crops. Make holes in a tin and put potato
and carrot peelings inside. Check your trap every so
often and burn the contents.

Wireworms

These are the larvae of the click beetle that are
mainly root eaters, particularly potatoes and carrots,
but also can trouble tomatoes, beans, peas, spinach,
kale, lettuce and others. They are most likely to
occur on vegetable plots recently transformed from
lawns. Don't cultivate roots for a couple of years
after grass has been growing, and use a millipede
trap to get rid of the wireworms if they are present.
Or gamma BHC.

Flea beetle

Another brassica enemy that nibbles away at the
leaves. Potatoes and radishes can also be plagued.
Wood ash helps to deter and derris should get rid of
it.

Onion fly

Perhaps the worst pest of all. Their maggots eat the
bulbs of onions. Sets and spring onions are usually
unaffected. Parsley and the smell of carrots grown
close by will also deter. Otherwise use
derris/pyrethrum or gamma BHC (Lindane).

Celery fly

The grubs of the celery fly cause brown leaf
blistering but can be prevented by a dusting of soot

146

in the rows before planting or a dose of nicotine or gamma BHC (Lindane), while blisters containing a maggot and appearing on the leaf will be Leaf Miners (see below).

Leaf Miner
Destroy grubs. Use a nicotine spray.

Mice
Can eat pea and bean seeds so dip them in paraffin before planting.

Thrips
The thrip larvae may get into pea pods. Lime will help deter them. Use pyrethrum or nicotine and burn affected plants.

Mealy bugs
Mealy cabbage aphis, attacking the underside of leaves of brassicas. Spray or dust with nicotine or derris.

Cutworms
These surface caterpillars eat the stems of lettuce, brassicas and sometimes tomatoes at ground level. Cardboard collars loosely tied round the stems will prevent this happening. Or proprietary baits.

Pea Moth
Will lay their eggs on the leaves of the pea and the maggots will enter the pod to feast on the peas. As flowers set spray with nicotine, but burn affected plants as soon as you spot them to prevent the spread.

Chafer
The grubs will damage potatoes and other roots so pick them out by hand or destroy with a nicotine solution whenever you come across them. Do not confuse with the friendly earthworm, although you shouldn't since chafers are bloated, dirty, whitish, evil-looking monsters.

Pets, birds and tempted neighbours
Netting, fencing, tin-foil strips and fists waved in the
air will usually do the trick.

DISEASES

Disease may be caused by viruses, bacteria or fungi.
But if your vegetables begin to show signs of an
ailment it may be caused by your own
mismanagement. Healthy plants, like people, have a
greater resistance to both pests and diseases, and
the surest way of keeping your vegetables in tip-top
condition is to provide them with the things they
need, when they need them, and in the right
amount. When they are grown indoors you will be
able to control their environment with regard to
lighting, temperature, food, humidity, water and
ventilation.

You can kill plants by kindness as much as by
neglect, as the deaths of many specimens murdered
by over-enthusiastic waterers testify. Too much of
one thing can actually be harmful when something
else is lacking in the environment since the growth
of plants is limited by whatever factor is available in
the smallest amount. The secret of successful
cultivation does not lie in the colour of your thumb
but in your ability to keep the right balance
between light, heat, water, humidity and ventilation,
and never to overcrowd vegetables even if you are
desperate for space. All risks of disease are
minimised when you grow the plants properly.

Hygiene is also crucial. Never leave bits of
rubbish, plant leaves, compost, thinnings and so on,
lying around. Thoroughly clean all containers before
re-using them by scrubbing them in hot water, and
rinsing out with boiling water.

Always use sterilised seed and potting compost
which will not carry any soil-borne disease. Buy
disease- and pest-resistant varieties of vegetables
where convenient to your overall plans. As a general
rule, the longer and more extensively a vegetable
has been cultivated in the country, the more likely it
will suffer from its own pests and diseases —

another good reason for choosing the more unusual
varieties for your indoor farm.

Although you may not feel inclined to actually
talk to them, get into the habit of giving all your
vegetables a daily looking over — check stem
wilting, leaf droop and discolouration, fruit moulds
and so on — and if you spot something wrong ask
whether there is some deficiency or excess in their
requirements that you have caused. Overwatering,
for example, could lead to stem or root rot, light
deficiency could mean weak, elongated stems, leaf
droop could arise from either too much or too little
water or too violent changes in temperature,
browning leaf tips may be the result of over-feeding
of draughts and yellowing leaves a sign of nutrient
deficiency.

Club Root
The curse of the brassica family, and a fungus
whose spores, up to 100,000 million of them under
every square metre of soil, get into the roots and
cause a smelly swelling. Prevent by crop rotation
(although club root can lie dormant in the ground
for twenty years or so), lime, improve the drainage,
don't leave the roots in the ground after they are
harvested, and raise in potting compost if at all
possible, transplanting to open ground with a good
ball of it adhering to the roots. Some people swear
by dropping a piece of rhubarb (or a mothball) into
the hole before planting to trick the fungus. Others
add a mix of boiled water and rhubarb leaves
(because of their poisonous oxalic acid content). If
you don't trust the more organic preventions, dip
roots in calomel before transplanting but bear in
mind that it is based on mercury. There is no cure
once club root strikes, so pull up and burn all
infected plants and don't use that ground for
brassicas for some years.

Leaf Spot
A form of botrytis (see later) which causes brown
marks on the leaves and stems of broad beans,
artichokes and celery in warm, humid weather.

Improve the drainage of the ground, add potash fertiliser (or wood ash) or buy seeds pre-treated with formaldehyde. Spray with Bordeaux mix (fairly harmless) or the slightly more potent Burgundy mix. Pull up and burn badly infected plants.

Stem Rot
May strike tomatoes, courgettes and cucumbers. Never overwater and avoid getting water on the stems.

Mosaic Virus
Causes yellow splodges and shrivelling of leaves of tomatoes and cucumbers. Greenfly carries the disease so attack them since there is no cure.

Potato Blight
Potato blight was to blame for the Irish potato famine in the 1840s. Your potatoes may still suffer, especially in hot, humid conditions. Rotate, buy resistant varieties where possible and use Bordeaux sprays. The disease is incurable. First signs are brown marks on the leaves and stems, then the foliage dies. Tubers have soft patches. Early varieties are less likely to be affected.

Verticillium Wilt
Another tomato fungus that cannot be cured except by increasing the temperature to just under 80 degrees for a couple of weeks, otherwise you must burn them. Look for signs of wilting and paling of the leaves after a coldish spell.

Tomato blight
Similar to the potato blight. Brown blotches on leaves and lumpy-looking fruit.

Mildew
Can lead to white/grey powdery patches forming on the leaves and stems of several vegetables, including peas, turnips, spinach, celery, artichoke, lettuce, marrow, onions, courgette, cucumber. Downy mildew causes yellowish, grey or purple mould on

the leaves of brassicas, onions and others. Good
drainage, proper spacing, correct rotation and good
ventilation help to prevent. Use Bordeaux or
Burgundy mix, or Thiram.

Halo Blight
Causes halo-like spots surrounded by a yellow ring
on the leaves of beans. Burn infected plants.

Rust
Affects the foliage of asparagus and should be dealt
with as mildew.

White Rot
This causes the leaves of onions to yellow and the
eventual rotting of the bulbs. Burn and do not use
the ground for several years.

Botrytis
Its symptoms may be grey mould forming on the
stems and leaves of lettuce and tomatoes, on soft
fruit, or neck or bulb rot in onions etc. Too humid
conditions, inadequate ventilation and overcrowding
may help cause it. Thiram or Dinocap should help
prevent it.

Parsnip Canker
These dark patches on the top of the root should be
avoided by buying a widely-available resistant
variety in the first place.

Celery Leaf Spot
Buy resistant varieties or rely on Bordeaux mix.

If you cannot identify the specific nature of a rot,
mould, blight, mildew or leaf, stem, root or fruit
blotches, you would be better off using a Bordeaux
spray than nothing at all. Buy disease resistant
varieties of vegetables wherever possible (as many
diseases are carried in the actual seed), and pay
careful attention to the actual growing environment
of your vegetables, particularly their watering,
temperature, and humidity, and do not overcrowd

them in containers. And if you do manage to 'save' a plant be sure you are not saving the disease, all ready to be passed on to others.

Whatever chemical you use against whatever pest and disease, do observe the golden rules of keeping everything well out of the reach of children, always using the correct amount as specified on the label, never inhaling the fumes, and avoid any contact with the skin, hair and especially the eyes. Never spray where there is food lying about, and direct the chemical to where it is needed rather than wave it around like an air freshener. Read the label twice.

Part Five
GROWING FRUIT

The main drawback to growing fruit indoors is that it probably won't get sufficient light and, if it does, the size of the bush will undoubtedly cast a shadow over the rest of your growing area and so limit the potential of the already limited spaces. Fruits also tend to take much longer to grow to maturity than vegetables.

The best place for fruit-growing on the small scale would be outdoors, on a sunny and sheltered patio or balcony perhaps. Without access to the great outdoors you could try fan training, or growing a fruit cordon, against the back wall of a sun lounge, keeping a dwarf fruit tree in a sunny corner of a room, or adapting a bay window area for melons and grapes.

Don't let this introduction to fruit-growing discourage you completely. By all means try it but keep a rein on your aspirations. It takes more than green fingers to change a city-block home into the garden of Eden.

Soft Fruits

Soft fruits are easy to grow and will yield handsomely in relation to the area they take up, provided you prune and train them carefully. They will happily fruit if grown from large tubs on a balcony or patio, or trained against walls and fences. Economise on space by planting single stem cordons if you can get them. Use John Innes potting compost No. 3, and protect all fruits against birds.

RASPBERRIES

Raspberries grow wild even in the wetter areas of Scotland, but, while being moisture-lovers, their growing medium must also be well drained to

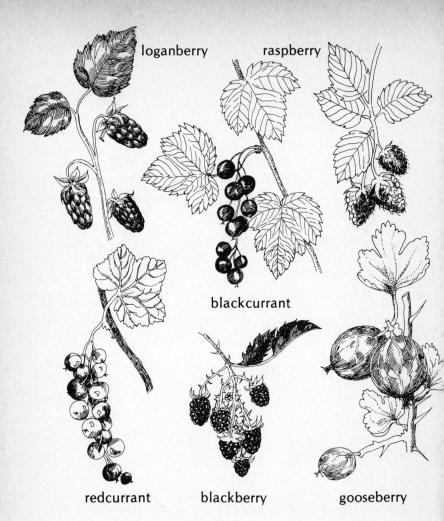

loganberry

raspberry

blackcurrant

redcurrant   blackberry   gooseberry

prevent water-logging and possible fungal disease.

Buy healthy, certified canes from a reputable
nursery to guarantee their freedom from virus
infection (for which there is no cure) and plant in
the winter to the same depth as the soil mark on the
cane. Raspberries will tolerate partial shade, and
like all soft fruits, they should be netted as a
protection against birds.

In the early spring cut back the cane to 6 inches
(to prevent fruiting in the first year and so
concentrate the cane's energies into building up a
strong root system). At the end of the first summer
cut away the original cane, and any feeble-looking

new ones, and loosely tie the rest to their supports.

In the late winter feed with a fertiliser containing plenty of potash. In the early spring cut the top 6 inches off the canes to encourage fruiting on the new shoots.

Watch for greenfly (which will spread dreaded virus) and also spray with derris when the flowers appear as a precaution against flea beetle and their maggots.

Pick the ripe berries but leave the cores, the green bit at the top of the berry that is part of the stem. After fruiting cut all the canes that bore fruit to ground level and reduce the rest to six good young growths per plant. Carry on in this way and you will be richly rewarded for the next ten years.

Varieties: Malling Jewel (freezes well), Glen Cova, September (for autumn fruiting).

LOGANBERRIES

One plant will provide plenty of fruit for a family of four but it will be harder to confine to a balcony or patio tub because of its spreading nature. You'll need wire netting against a wall or a trellis to spread the canes. They will flourish, as do blackberries, without much sunshine.

Plant the canes in winter as deep as the soil mark and firm down well. Cut back to 12 inches. Fruiting takes place on the previous year's canes, so the new canes must be tied together out of the way, usually in the middle of the fanned out fruiting canes. The old ones are cut out after fruiting and the new ones take their place on the support. Fan them out to leave the centres open for the following year's canes.

In all other respects loganberries should be treated like raspberries (although since birds fancy them less, they possibly won't have to be netted). They, too, will fruit for many blissful years.

Varieties are known by their numbers: LY59, L654 (thornless).

BLACKBERRIES

Since there are plenty of wild ones to be had in the country towards the end of the summer it hardly seems worth bothering with blackberries. But if you are too town-bound for such excursions, or would like to sample a more refined class of blackberry, even without thorns, grow your own. And do so in more or less the same way as loganberries.

Varieties: Oregon Thornless, Merton Thornless.

BLACKCURRANTS

Blackcurrants (red and white too) are good yielders, producing about ten pounds per bush. They will grow in partial shade but do take up quite a bit of space, more than a cordon of redcurrants.

Buy a two-year-old certified plant from a reputable nursery and put it in its place in the early winter. Blackcurrants should be planted a little deeper than the soil mark. Cut back in the early spring to leave just 3 buds. The tub should be well draining and stood in a corner protected from the wind. Feed well with liquid manure and water regularly.

You must prune the bush to prevent overcrowding, control the shape of the bush (or the direction of growth in the case of cordons) and the replacement of new shoots for old. About one third of your blackcurrant bush should be removed each year. Cut away poor looking shoots and old branches to a new shoot. Your nurseryman will be glad to show you just what to do when you buy the plant.

Protect blackcurrants against 'big bud' mites and leaf scorch by spraying with lime sulphur.

Varieties: Baldwin, Wellington XXX.

REDCURRANTS

Most of what we have said about blackcurrants will

apply to red. They are pruned differently since fruit grows on the two-year-old shoots. Or grow as a ready-pruned cordon against even a north facing wall. Feed with a high potash general fertiliser at the beginning of the year. Don't let the birds get to the fruits before you do.

Varieties: Red Lake, Laxtons No. 1 (whitecurrants: White Grape).

GOOSEBERRIES

Follow the rules for redcurrants. Watch for birds, and still more birds, and, as a precaution against American gooseberry mildew, spray with a mix of ¼ lb of washing soda to a gallon of water. Or use Dinocap. Use derris against sawfly.

Varieties: Careless, Langley Gage, Lancashire Lad. Or try the new Cape gooseberry, or golden berry, with the apricoty taste.

Melons

Melons will grow indoors if they can be given plenty of sunshine, and could transform a south-facing bay window into a truly exotic indulgence. And a money saver too, considering the high cost of shop-bought melons even at their low seasonal prices. They will take up quite a bit of space though.

The Cantaloupe hybrids are the least demanding, or try the new mini varieties such as Ha-Ogen which will produce around ten fruits per plant. Both will need to be trained on a strong support of wires, about 10 inches apart in a window or patio/balcony greenhouse, and the fruits may need to be held by nets. If you grow melons on the flat in a cold frame, trailing along the ground, you should put a piece of wood under each fruit to prevent rotting from their contact with damp compost.

Sow each melon seed on its edge, ¼ inch deep in a 3 inch peat pot in the middle of spring. They

should be propagated at a temperature of 70 degrees — this heat is a very important factor in their ability to germinate. As soon as the seed does germinate give it plenty of light, and when 3 inches high transplant to a 5 or 6 inch pot (filled with John Innes compost No. 2). Later pot on to a 12 inch pot (John Innes No. 3, and a bottom layer of organic compost if possible) or put two in a grow-bag. Melons grow best in a daytime temperature between 65 and 70 degrees fahrenheit, and a night-time minimum of 55 degrees.

Their general cultivation requirements are similar to cucumbers. Give them plenty of ventilation and a syringe with a fine mist sprayer two or three times a day. Restrict the side shoots at two leaves beyond each fruit, aiming to produce four or five melons on each plant, and pinch out the non-bearing laterals five leaves from the main stem. Pollinate the female flowers (behind which the melon can be seen developing) by brushing pollen from the male flowers with a camel hair brush, or pollinate as for courgettes. Do it on a dry, warm day.

Give melons plenty of water, especially once the fruits have begun to set, and stop when they stop swelling. You should support the fruits of the larger varieties by nets. Always keep water away from the stem to avoid collar rot. Feed every so often with liquid high-potash fertiliser. To test for ripeness squeeze the end with your thumb — they should be ready around late summer.

Strawberries

For sheer palate pleasure it's hard to beat a ripe, juicy strawberry. They are full of vitamin C, and smell good too.

Grow them indoors in pots, barrels, special strawberry urns, tower pots, suspended polythene sleeves of specially prepared compost, or from hanging baskets. Buy the plants directly from a reputable supplier and ask for disease-free stock (to minimise the chances of the fruit suffering from hereditary virus disease). Plant in mid to late summer — if you leave it till later or the spring you should remove the flowers to prevent their fruiting in the first year. Otherwise hand-pollinate to get the maximum crop. If you buy plants through the mail unpack, expose to light and plant without delay. Alpine strawberries should be raised from seed (they do not produce 'runners' like ordinary strawberries) early in the year in a temperature around 55 degrees.

If you are using one of the multi-pocket urns, fill the container to the level of the first opening with potting compost and put a plant in the hole. Then add more compost, firming down as you go, till it reaches the level of the next opening and plant the second one. Continue in this way till you fill the container and crown it with one or two more.

If you have access to a patch of outdoors it would be well worth constructing a simple strawberry panel so that the fruits will grow vertically and take up a negligible amount of room. The panel can be of any convenient height, and about six inches across. Make a wooden frame (the sides of the panel can be sloped so that they get the maximum benefit from the sun) and cover the sides with chicken wire. Line the inside with black plastic, then fill it up with potting compost. Make holes in the plastic and the compost for the plants to fit in.

Don't water strawberries to excess but do increase the dose when the fruit begins to set. Spray regularly

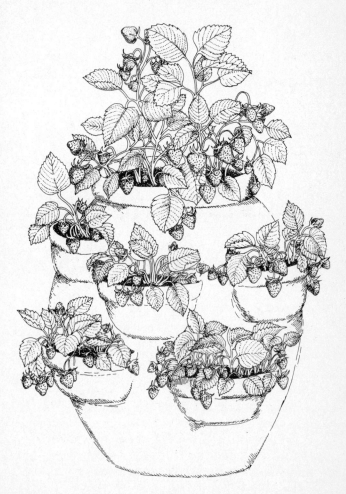

to increase humidity, but also provide a well-ventilated atmosphere. After flowering give the plants a weekly feed with liquid fertiliser, and assist pollination of indoor-grown strawberries with a camel-hair brush. Remove any runners that appear.

Birds and slugs enjoy strawberries, and aphids can carry virus disease. If the atmosphere is too warm and humid botrytis (grey mould) may strike.

Harvest your crop in the summer and cut back the foliage after fruiting so that the plants may crop again (but treat Alpines as annuals — Cambridge Favourite is a popular variety).

Grapes

The idea that grapes will only thrive in sun-drenched regions of the world is nonsense. Their cultivation in England is basically a question of choosing a

suitable variety and growing-method. That isn't meant to imply that a vine can be pushed away in some dim corner of a living room and expected to flourish. Unless you have a sheltered south-facing outdoor spot, you must allocate a sunny bay window, a sun lounge or balcony greenhouse for vine culture, and since these are the most cherished areas for many other vegetables, you may decide that grapes aren't all that important to you after all. They don't like sharing space with other crops.

A 12 inch-plus pot can be home to six or seven bunches a year. Buy a one-year-old plant from a nursery or vineyard during the late autumn and plant in John Innes compost No. 3. Stick two 4 foot bamboo canes into the pot, and secure a smaller cane between the two. These will be used to train the vine along. After planting cut back the cane to leave three buds.

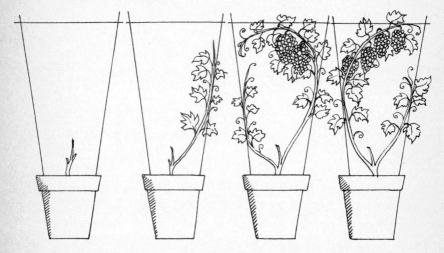

In the spring allow one of the buds, the strongest looking, to grow and cut back the other two. But don't let it develop fruit-bearing lateral shoots until its third year as this abstinence will let the vine develop a strong root system. Prune back to three buds again the following winter, and then allow two to grow in the spring, one of which will bear fruit and can be trained along one of the bamboo canes, and the other, trained along the second, will be its replacement. In the first year of fruiting, the third year of the vine's growth, restrict the number of fruit bearing laterals to two, pinching out the growing tip two leaves beyond a bunch. Stop non-

fruiting laterals at four leaves, and sub-laterals
(those growing from laterals) at one leaf. Allow an
extra two bunches each year. That will be hard to
do but will pay dividends in later years. In the winter
cut away the arm that bore the fruit and the other
one will take its place for the following year. Next
spring allow another replacement cane to develop in
the same way. And if all that sounds rather
complicated, it is. Ask you friendly nurseryman if
you feel you need more advice.

Grape vines enjoy sunshine but never excessive
heat, so always make sure that the room where it
grows is well ventilated. Water sparingly and stop
when the grapes start to swell. Dessert grapes should
have their bunches thinned out to give those
remaining grapes swelling room. Syringe when the
fruit appears and tap the flowering vine daily to
assist pollination. Spray with Bordeaux mixture as a
precaution against mildew. Try Black Hamburgh for
an indoor variety in a cool room.

Citrus fruits

Seedsman-reared citrus plants are hard to come by in
England, apart from those miniature orange trees
which produce tiny fruits that are not really edible
beyond flavouring a party punch-bowl.

Unfortunately the task of growing a fruit-bearing
tree from a pip shouldn't be underestimated. They
are difficult to germinate; if they do germinate they
may not bloom; if they bloom they do not always
set fruit; and if they do fruit they may not be 'true'
to their type, and probably not too enjoyable. But
try. Even if it fails to produce food you will at least
have quite a spectacular house plant with the
promise of one day becoming productive.

Start off pips in a peat pot and later re-pot,
ending up in a big 18 inch pot or tub. Should pips
fail try 'rooting' a side shoot by planting it in a pot
filled with a mixture of sand and peat sealed in a
plastic bg till it looks well established or obtain
special varieties from a specialist nursery. A citrus

163

tree grown indoors should be kept in the sunniest position, in a well ventilated bay window, sun lounge, or patio greenhouse, and rotated so that all sides get their share of sunshine. Keep the tree to a maximum of four feet, assuming you have the patience to let it get that tall, water well, with tepid water, and provide a humid atmosphere. Stand it in a shower every so often.

Tree fruits

You won't have room for an orchard. Self-fertile apple, pear and peach trees, on the other hand, are fairly widely obtainable in dwarf varieties, suitable for growing in pots and tubs on balconies and patios. Don't even attempt to grow them from seed, but buy your tree from a garden centre. It will already be trained into a basic shape (and so will cordons if you decide they would be better suited to your growing area, trained against a wall even on quite narrow strips between, say, a door and a window). You will have to prune to maintain that original shape and allow plenty of light to reach the middle. Your nurseryman will advise you on how to prune your choice of fruit tree — and perhaps sell you a specialist's book on the subject.

Part Six
AND THEN . . .

A Guide to Herbs

Herbs have been grown for all sorts of reasons — to look decorative, smell fragrant, cure ailments, feed skin and hair, and to make love and magic — but it is for their culinary use that they are commonly grown in homes and gardens, to flavour and garnish food. They can change the taste of a dish as distinctly as its basic ingredients.

While their natural habitat is the coastal regions of the Mediterranean, most herbs will flourish indoors with a fair amount of light, be it natural or artificial. Grow a selection of several different kinds, rather than too much of a few. They can be grown in almost any sort of container, from pots to window boxes, and they are particularly suited to strawberry or tower pots in which each herb can grow out of its own individual pocket. A kitchen sill is a most convenient place — just reach over and snip whenever you need them. But avoid overcrowding, especially as some herbs are particularly sensitive about touching the leaves of another.

The majority of the herbs you are likely to want to grow will be perennials, cropping every year (as opposed to annuals which bloom and die in one growing season). They can be grown either from cuttings, perhaps taken from a friend's herb garden, or from seedlings bought from a nursery. Replace them every third year, and at the same time change the potting compost in which they grow. Annuals should be sown as seeds, in the same way as vegetables, ¼ inch deep, and thinned to 6 inches apart or transplanted to an 8 inch pot. As a rule seed-raised herbs take quite a time to germinate, especially parsley. Some herbs can also be bought pre-sown in their own mini greenhouse containers.

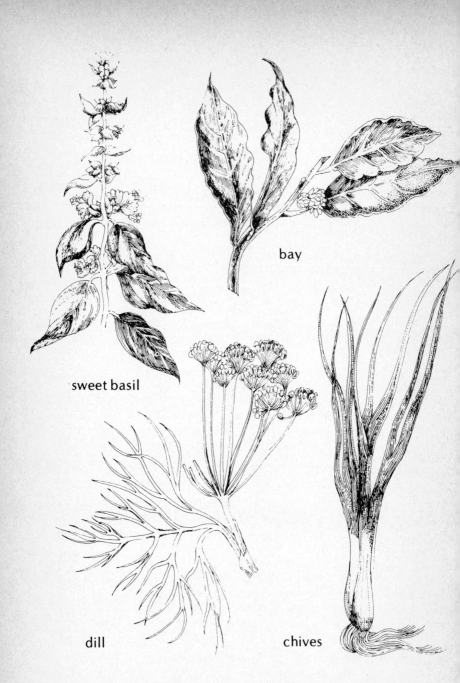

sweet basil

bay

dill

chives

Just moisten their compost and place on a sunny window ledge, and later transplant to their final containers.

166

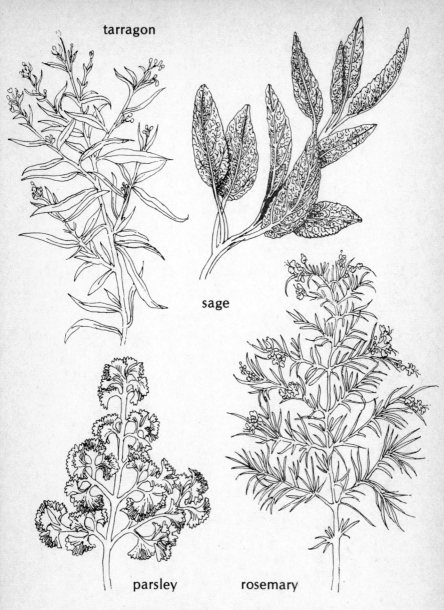

tarragon

sage

parsley   rosemary

Water herbs from above, or let them soak up water from a pan, but never overwater. They grow naturally in light, poorish, fast draining soils. Syringe occasionally to keep dust and other city grime off the foliage, and give them an occasional meal of liquid fertiliser.

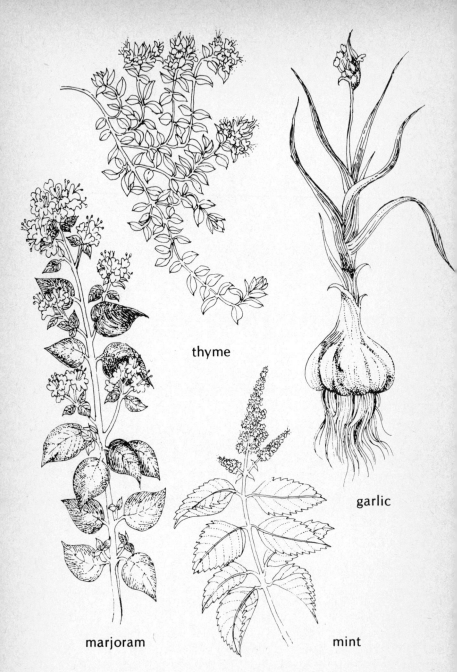

thyme

garlic

marjoram

mint

Should you discover that your harvest is too
bountiful for your own immediate needs, and many
herbs will flourish the more you cut them, you can

always dry them and give away as presents, perhaps in bouquet garni or fines herbes collections. To dry herbs pick them before they flower (and in the morning, after the dew has dried, if you are growing them in an outside area or window box). Spread out on a cake or oven grid and put them in a low oven with the door left open for a few minutes. Or tie in bunches by the stems and hang in a cool, well ventilated place, out of direct sunlight, to dry naturally. Either way they will crackle to the touch when dry. Or they can be frozen.

The following list of herbs is only a suggestion. Don't be afraid to experiment with your own favourites, but check with your supplier first to see if they will make any unusual demands.

BASIL, SWEET

A sun worshipper, so don't relegate to anywhere but a south-facing window area. It is an annual, so grow it from seed, although it can live for two or three years.

Basil is a vital ingredient in most tomato dishes, especially pasta sauces, but is well suited to many other vegetable dishes, including courgettes, carrots, beans, peas and mushrooms. Pop some into stews too, and add sparingly to salads and cheese dishes since it is a strong taster. Basil forms the basis of Italian pesto sauce. Use pesto on pasta. Medically it is used, among other remedies, for bites and stings.

BAY

Bay can be grown as a miniature tree in a balcony tub or on a patio. Bring it indoors during the winter for warmth, easy snippings and a conversation piece. Its leaves are, or should be, rich green, and if you want to retain that colour they should be dried in the dark.

Bay leaves make an important addition to nearly all stews and a few soups. Better used dried than fresh.

CHIVES

A member of the onion family, but cultivated for its stalks instead of the roots. It is wiser to buy the plants from a nurseryman as it takes two years for seed-grown chives to become lush enough for cutting. Grow about three clumps to make it worthwhile. Cut regularly to prevent flowering and to stimulate further growth. Chives will feel comfortable in partial shade. A dressing with liquid fertiliser now and then will encourage it along.

Chives have the flavour of very mild onions. Add some to scrambled egg and omelettes, and to any salads, especially potato or tomato salad. It will also fare well with cheese dishes and sweet corn, and don't forget chive butter for meat grills.

DILL

Dill is an annual, grown from seed in peat pots and subsequently transferred to a pot or the window box, the one with the nearest to a southern

Mediterranean climate. Thin to 9 inches apart and keep moist. The foliage is beautiful. When the flowers have set, cut the plant, hang it upside down to dry in the usual way but wrap a bag round it to collect the seeds as they fall.

The seeds are crucial for flavouring dill pickles and vinegars. You can also use the leaves for enhancing the taste of salads, fish sauces, and mixed with butter for tender new vegetables, especially potatoes.

GARLIC

This is really an onion not a herb, and is a perennial. Plant a clove, an ordinary one from the greengrocer, in a pot of compost so that the tip is just sticking up above the surface, and firm down the compost. Only water garlic when the compost becomes very dry, and give it plenty of light. When the leaves begin to yellow at the end of the summer lift the bulbs and hang in a warm place, perhaps near a kitchen boiler, to dry. Keep them strung up in bunches, like an onion seller's onions. It should keep vampires away.

Not everybody likes garlic, or the other way around. You should always use it sparingly as it is strong and can easily dominate the rest of the meal. Use it in casseroles and stews. Rub a clove round the inside of a salad bowl before preparing a salad. It is also used for pickling. And it is good for you. Turn a French loaf into garlic bread by slicing it almost to the base, spreading on a mixture of crushed garlic, pre-softened butter, parsley (thyme and marjoram too if you like), salt and pepper, and wrap everything tightly in tin foil. Bake in a medium oven for about twenty minutes and serve hot.

MARJORAM, POT

The English equivalent of Italian oregano, and very fragrant. It is a perennial and, since seed-raising is a slow business, buy a seedling. Remove the leaves from the top of the plant to prevent blossoming,

171

and syringe frequently.

Oregano is an all purpose herb that most famously appears in tomato-based dishes, notably Neapolitan sauces and pizzas. Use marjoram in the same way. It also works well with most meats, especially sausages, stews and stuffings. Add it to the following vegetables: cauliflower, courgettes, peas, mushrooms, cooked celery, potatoes, spinach, aubergine, greens and carrots, as well as tomatoes. Tea infusions can help relieve upset stomachs and get rid of bad breath (caused by too much garlic?).

MINT

Mint is a perennial that is easier to grow than to stop. Just take a cutting, put it in water in a light place, and transfer to a pot as soon as the roots develop. Never plant mint in a window box or anywhere else in the company of other growing things because its roots will soon begin a grand take-over bid. Mint requires little attention beyond an occasional watering, and it will flourish in the shade. Its smell is very distinctive, and there are several different varieties to choose from, the most popular being spearmint, peppermint and apple (or Bowles) mint.

Mint's most traditional employment is as a sauce for lamb, and as a marinade for kebabs. Its flavour will also suit carrots, beans, peas and potatoes, and vanilla ice cream. Use it for making mint julep, with brandy, sugar and ice. Freeze chopped-up leaves in ice cubes to give your cold drinks a refreshing appeal. Tea infusions are prescribed by herbalists for sore mouths, and by Moroccans for relaxation. Peppermint is supposed to counteract migraine and even heighten virility.

PARSLEY

A biennial that is best grown from seed in the early spring. Exceedingly slow to germinate, taking between five and six weeks, but you can speed things up by soaking the seeds in water for 24 hours before sowing. If you are impatient by nature, buy seedlings. Grow the dwarf curly varieties indoors from a hanging basket in the kitchen window (which needn't face south since parsley prefers partial shade) or in a proper parsley pot. In a window box you could intercrop radishes at the same time as they will be ready for pulling before the parsley sprouts. Keep moist, pinch off the blooms, and re-grow every two years.

Parsley is full of vitamins, particularly C. It most commonly appears in parsley sauce, served over white fish dishes, but a parsley omelette takes a lot of beating. Use it with peas, artichokes, corn, turnips, mushrooms, potatoes, tomatoes, and widely in salad dishes.

ROSEMARY

A perennial which can either be grown from a cutting in the late autumn, or raised from a garden centre plant (you could try growing from seed but they are slow to germinate). In the spring the herb will produce attractive pale blue flowers. Rosemary prefers a cool but sunnyish position, and quite a bit of space. Never let it dry out (but do not overwater — it needs a well drained soil) and occasionally feed with liquid fertiliser. Syringe the undersides of the leaves as a precaution against red spider mite.

With beautiful fragrance and looks to boot, rosemary is used to flavour strong tasting foods, such as game, some fishes, roast lamb, beef casseroles and minestrone. It also adds an exciting flavour to vegetables, such as roast potatoes, spinach and cabbage. If you have trouble getting to sleep at night, make a cup of rosemary tea.

SAGE

Sage is a perennial, and an evergreen. Grow from cuttings in the early spring, or buy a widely available nursery plant. Nip out the growing tips to encourage bushiness and syringe to prevent red spider mite.

Another powerful taster to be used gently in stuffings, sausages, patés and roasts. Also add in mini-pinch proportions to eggs, cheese, aubergine and whatever you fancy.

TARRAGON, FRENCH

Grow this perennial from cuttings or buy ready-raised plants. It likes a dryish, well-drained soil and an occasional syringe, but very little else in the way of attention.

Tarragon is a pleasant-smelling herb that is widely used in cooking. Use a little at a time, and add towards the end of any lengthy cooking operations. Used with many vegetables, and to flavour chicken salads, various sauces (particularly béarnaise), hamburgers and so on. To make tarragon vinegar, or any herb vinegar come to that (rosemary, thyme, basil, dill), soak the leaves and stalks in wine or cider vinegar, add a clove of garlic, lemon peel, and perhaps some cloves and raisins, and keep well corked for two or three weeks. Strain and bottle the liquid. Add tarragon to olive oil too.

THYME

There are lots of different varieties of this perennial, but lemon and common garden thyme are the two to be recommended. Buy a plant or grow from cuttings taken from top growth, and ideally add a touch of lime or ground chalk to its growing compost. Prune to keep bushy.

A strong herb, used with cottage and cream cheese, sea foods and stuffings, and to accompany broccoli, turnips, aubergine, beets, carrots, leeks and onions. Thyme tea, sweetened with honey, is a great comforter for cold and sore throat sufferers. Also an important part of any bouquet garni, together with parsley, celery, marjoram, a hint of rosemary and a bay leaf, all tied up together in a piece of cheesecloth. 'Mixed herbs' are a mêlée of thyme, sage, parsley and tarragon.

Mushrooms

Every home has enough mush-room. Although rarely credited for being particularly nutritious, mushrooms in fact surpass many other fruits and vegetables in their food value (measured on a dry weight basis).

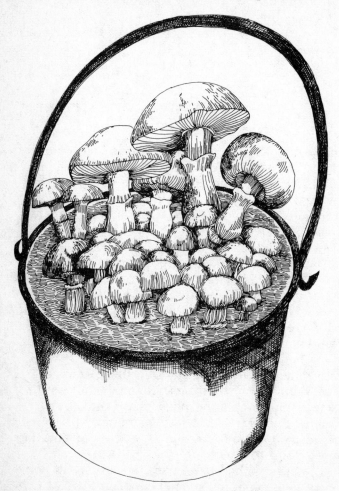

They contain, among other health-giving properties, folic acid for the blood and, being starch free, they can form a tasty addition to a weight watcher's diet programme.

Mushrooms are a fungus, not a vegetable. They do not photosynthesise and so can grow quite happily

in the dark. A crop of mushrooms in your indoor
farm can therefore convert the most obscure places,
such as cellars, attics, cupboards under the stairs,
beneath a sink unit, and even directly under your
bed, into a productive area. Don't underestimate
their yield — each square foot can produce well
over a pound of mushrooms.

Whatever way you choose to grow them,
mushrooms will need a temperature between 50 and
60 degrees, all the year round, if you want all the
year round cropping. Beyond the extremes of 48 and
68 degrees mushrooms simply cannot grow, but if
the temperature should temporarily fall below this
don't be alarmed. Your mushrooms will just bide
their time in a dormant state till things start to
warm up. The air must be fairly moist, but not the
excessively damp atmosphere that many people
believe to be ideal, and well ventilated, with plenty
of fresh air but never draughts, and avoid exposing
mushrooms to direct sunlight.

The best method of growing mushrooms at home
is *not* by committing yourself to one of the various
'schemes' you see advertised, promising you a
second income or an early retirement on the
proceeds, and a guarantee to buy back your crops
at a fixed price.

Instead, send off for one, or several, of the pre-
sown mushroom packs offered by some of the big

seed companies in their annual catalogues, or now sold in some of the larger chain-stores. The kits, usually packed in plastic buckets contain pre-sown mushroom spawn that will produce several crops, or 'flushes', of mushrooms over a long period. And without any smell or mess. The kits come with complete instructions — you have to do very little beyond a bit of 'casing' spreading, the regular moistening and final picking.

Mushroom growing by alternative methods will present rather a problem unless you have a backyard in which to prepare the compost, or a nurseryman who is willing to sell it to you already prepared. The ultimate success of a mushroom crop is very dependent on the composting process being carried out properly, and there are no short cuts.

Mushrooms, or rather the mycelium (the 'rooting' system), grow best on horse manure (or poultry, though less well) that has been composted on wheat, barley or rye straw. To obtain such supplies you would have to collect it from, say, a riding stable whose horses have been bedded on straw (many aren't — several use sawdust for example which is far less satisfactory for mushroom growing).

A thirty square-foot, 9 inches deep, growing area will require about 5 hundredweight of straw mixed with horse manure, or 2 hundredweight of straw and about 22 pounds of poultry manure. Alternatively you can buy a special mushroom compost supplement that acts as an activator in the breaking down of the straw in place of manure. Either way the preparation of the compost is a messy, smelly and space-consuming business. Basically you must first thoroughly saturate the straw with water and then build up a heap, alternating a thick layer of straw with a thin layer of activator, in a similar way as ordinary garden composts are prepared. The heap must be continually turned, outside to centre, so that the whole pile heats up, and kept moist. Gypsum is usually added to prevent greasiness. After a few weeks of weekly turnings and keeping moist the compost should be rich brown, without smell, and ready for use. Apart from the actual scale of mushroom growing that such a compost heap makes possible, this richly organic material is an excellent source of humus for your garden if you have one, or your garden compost pile.

You will need several 9 inch deep boxes to put the compost and spawn in. Make them or use old fish or fruit crates, lined with polythene. Fix wooden 'legs' to each of the corners so that they will stack about 9 inches above one another and enable you to cram as much square footage into a limited space as possible. On a smaller scale an unwanted tea trolley or bookshelf area could be adapted to mushroom growing.

Wait until the temperature of the compost has fallen below 80 degrees before filling the boxes. Firm it down well. The compost should be changed three times a year, but make sure the boxes are thoroughly cleaned out with boiling water before re-filling, and as a general precaution against mushroom ailments, dust the beds with pyrethrum.

When the temperature of the compost has dropped below 70 degrees, spread dry mushroom grain spawn over the surface, working it into the compost to a depth of about 1 or 2 inches. If you use manure spawn it should be broken into ¾ inch lumps and pushed 2 inches into the compost, 10 inches apart. Keep the compost moist (or cover the boxes with black polythene sheeting or damp newspaper to retain moisture).

When the spawn begins to absorb moisture, the mycelium no longer remains dormant. Its fine white threads will thicken up and expand, or 'run', into the surrounding compost in search of food. The mushroom itself is the fruiting head of the mycelium.

After two or three weeks you should apply a covering, or 'casing', of moistened peat (often mixed with chalk) to a depth of just over an inch. This casing will support the growing mushrooms. Use a fine mist sprayer to keep the casing constantly moist but do not overwater at this stage because the water should not reach the compost below as it may kill the spawn.

About three weeks later the mushrooms should appear, and will be fully mature about two weeks after that. They will grow in clumps, appearing in waves or 'flushes' over a two or three month period, perhaps longer. Leave them until they open before picking as they will taste better. When picking twist up and out of the compost and cut off the very end of the stalk. Carefully remove any remaining bits of mushroom from the compost before refilling the holes with casing as they could spoil the rest of the crop.

Eat your mushrooms raw, perhaps marinated for a couple of hours beforehand in two parts oil to one part lemon juice.

Don't wash or peel mushrooms as you wash and peel a lot of the goodness away — just wipe them with a damp cloth. Cook them fast and furiously by sautéing in a pan.

Sprouting Seeds

Most people, at some time in their lives, grow mustard and cress. Apart from being a worthy foundation for future indoor farming activities—an initial trial run at growing your own food in your home—mustard and cress can always make a valuable contribution from the younger members of

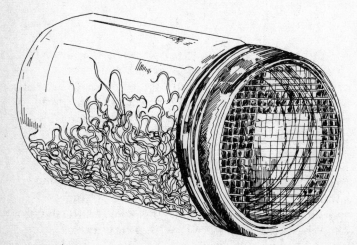

the family after you've moved on to other sprouting seeds.

A vast range of other seeds can be sprouted, and all of them can be tucked away into a cupboard farm without competing with any of the other indoor crops for space, light or much of your time. Sprouting seeds can even flourish in a drawer, making them a perfect ingredient for an office-grown lunch.

Germinating seeds have an extremely high nutritional value, far more, in relation to their size, than their fully grown plant. Half a cup of sprouted alfalfa, for example, is the vitamin C equivalent of six glasses of pure orange juice.

The range to choose from is enormous:

Mung beans (the Chinese restaurant type)	Fennel
Kidney beans	Celery
Alfalfa	Soya
Lima beans	Mustard
Lentils	Cress
Chick peas	Adzuki
Sunflower seeds	Buckwheat
Wheat	Barley
Peas	Corn
Fenugreek	Oats
Radishes	Millet
Triticale	Pumpkin
Lettuce	Peanut

. . . and so on. *But you must buy seeds that are for sprouting not sowing,* as the latter are often chemically treated. So your choice of what to sprout will effectively be limited by the supplies stocked by your local health food store, enlightened garden centre or seedsman.

All seeds can be sprouted in the mustard and cress way. Lay either a thickish layer of paper towels, flannel, cotton wool, dish cloth, towelling or similar material in a shallow pan or dish and thoroughly moisten. Sprinkle the seeds fairly thickly over the surface and cover with a tight cover, such as tin foil, or slide the tray into a polythene bag, seal the end, and put newspaper over the top to keep out the light. When they begin to sprout, after a couple of days, give them light, but not direct sunlight. Re-moisten the base if necessary, but avoid soaking it or the seeds may turn mouldy.

Remember, when growing mustard and cress, to sow the cress four days before the mustard as it is slower to germinate and you might want to enjoy the two together. They will then both be ready to

eat in about two weeks.

You can also sprout seeds by the jar method, using large ones such as preserving jars. Punch lots of holes in the lids, or cover the tops with pieces of cheesecloth or nylon gauze, securing them to the jars with elastic bands.

Fill the jars about a quarter full with the seeds (less for the smaller seeds like alfalfa as they will expand by up to ten times their original size). Replace the tops on the jars. Wash the seeds thoroughly through the lid perforations in tepid water (larger seeds like mung beans can be left to soak overnight to speed up their germination). Shake the jar vigorously and drain off all the water. Leave to stand overnight and repeat the washing and draining process morning and night for the next few days until the sprouts are ready to be eaten. Make sure you don't miss a bath, and always drain well; too much water can rot the seeds, and too little will court crop failure. Don't waste the drained water — use it on your other vegetables as it will be nutritious.

Seeds sprout best in a warm room, with the temperature fairly constant around 65 degrees. Sprouting time will depend on the seed, but in general they will be ready to eat in less than a week. Don't overgrow them or they will begin to taste bitter, and don't eat the seeds if they fail to germinate.

Eat the sprouts — hulls and all — raw, either on their own as a salad, mixed with other salad crops, or added to muesli for breakfast. They will enhance any sandwich, and can also be popped into soup or omelettes. You can boil them, but never for longer than a couple of minutes, or stir fry them for a minute, and then perhaps simmer them in soy sauce, Chinese style, for a further five. They can be added to stews and even bread. Or just leave a bowlful on the table to nibble away at.

Maintaining a constant supply of health-making sprouts throughout the year is one of the simplest and most beneficial things you could do for yourself, your family and friends.

Yoghurt

Since yoghurt is a valuable food, and one that you actually grow by the propagation of bacteria cultures, it is most worthy of shelf space in any indoor farm.

The secret of yoghurt making is to establish just the right conditions for the bacteria cultures to reproduce and spread through milk, so turning it into yoghurt.

Start off by first boiling the milk, to make it sterile, and letting it cool till it is lukewarm (between 100 and 120 degrees fahrenheit, finger-dipping good — a dairy thermometer would be useful). Pour the yoghurt culture, or live yoghurt, into the milk and stir well with a wooden spoon. Use roughly a tablespoon of culture to every pint of milk.

The simplest way to make yoghurt is to use a thermos flask to retain the warmth of the milk. Pour the mixture into the flask, replace the lid, and leave it to sit undisturbed for a few hours. Alternatively, you could use ordinary lidded jars and stand them in a larger pot filled with heated water. The water in the outer container can have its temperature held fairly constant either by adding hot water as the existing water begins to cool, or standing the whole thing in a pre-heated oven. If you're the type of person who needs a kitchen full of gadgetry before boiling an egg, buy a special yoghurt-making machine.

Whatever way you make yoghurt, don't jog the yog as the cultures are very sensitive to disturbances.

After a few hours remove the yoghurt, cool and refrigerate. Eat with fruit, nuts or whatever you fancy, but save some to start the next batch.

Part Seven

AFTER THE HARVEST

Cooking Your Vegetables and Fruit

Vegetables really suffer, in flavour, texture and goodness, if they are overcooked. It seems rather a pointless exercise to care about growing vegetables to perfection if they are not to be cooked with the same diligence.

In the first place you should harvest your crops while they are still young and tender. There is no virtue whatsoever in cultivating whoppers, except as a boast to your neighbours. Pull, pick or cut the vegetables only when you are ready to eat them, either raw in a salad or cooked. If you find they are ripening faster than you can devour them you should still pick when young and tender and store in that state until you are ready to enjoy them.

Preparation should be thorough but never taken to excess. Scrub, rather than peel, your roots wherever possible as their most nutritious part lies directly beneath the skin. Wash vegetables fast and furiously and never leave them drowning in a bowl of water.

If they are not to be enjoyed in their raw state, vegetables should be cooked for the minimum amount of time, just enough for them to become tender. If you boil the vegetables use only a shallow amount of salted water, perhaps with a touch of lemon juice added, and add them after the water has come to the boil. Steaming is preferable to boiling as the goodness of the vegetables doesn't escape into the water (although the cooking water should be used as a base for stocks or soups, or for watering your growing crops after it has cooled). Invest in a steaming basket, the type that will fit inside different shapes and sizes of saucepan. Pressure cookers will also treat your vegetables well, particularly the tougher ones, but your timing must be accurate as every second counts in this intensive method of steaming.

Don't overlook the various other ways of cooking vegetables: sauté or stir fry, fritter or fry in batter, bake, grill or roast. A good vegetable cookbook will supply you with an indispensable source of ideas. And use your herbs — the guide to herbs on pp. 165-174 will help you decide which goes best with what.

The simplest way of eating fruit is straight from its bush, vine or tree, but you may feel that your growing efforts deserve a more refined preparation and presentation of the fruits of your labour. So add a little cream and sugar or your own yoghurt. There are thousands of dessert and pudding recipes that most general cookbooks seem to boast, from tarts and trifles to flans and fools, not forgetting pies, crumbles, stewed fruits and even the soufflé. Don't forget fruit in the morning, on cereals of all kinds, especially health-making muesli.

SOUPS

Soup making is the perfect excuse for experimenting and juggling around with a variety of ingredients, combining vegetables, herbs and starchy bits (pasta, lentils, pearl barley and so on) till you have worked a culinary miracle or two.

A blender is a worthwhile buy, but a mouli mixer or an ordinary sieve or large strainer will do. Use either your vegetable cooking water (which can also be reduced and made into a sauce) or vegetable peelings, which are crammed with goodness, as a base. Dice and add your vegetables and other ingredients, plus seasoning, and simmer the lot. Don't overcook — the vegetables need to be soft, but not mushy, so add potatoes before peas for example. If you want a clear soup strain off the liquid. For soft soups put everything in a blender, or through the mouli or sieve. Add milk or cream, for cream soups, stirring well to avoid scorching the milk or cream, just before serving. You could top with sliced French bread and cheese, and put into a moderate oven for fifteen minutes. Or just add a few crispy fried bread croûtons.

VINAIGRETTE DRESSING

Since much of your home produce will be eaten raw, here is a basic salad dressing to flatter them with:

6 tbsp olive oil
2 tbsp white wine vinegar (and/or lemon juice)
¼ tsp mustard powder or French mustard
Salt and pepper
Pinch of sugar

Mix together the vinegar, lemon juice, mustard, sugar, salt and pepper. Add oil gradually, beating it with a fork as you do. Add herbs to taste (tarragon, chives, parsley). Toss all together with salad before serving. For a stronger dressing add garlic and/or Moutarde de Meaux (or any other kind of mustard) in whatever quantities you like.

RATATOUILLE

1 onion
1 aubergine
1 pepper
2 courgettes
small cucumber
2 cloves garlic
1 small chili pepper
4 tbsp olive oil
6 tbsp vinaigrette sauce
2 tsp sugar
black pepper
2 peeled tomatoes
small tin tomato purée (make your own)
½ pint vegetable broth

Finely chop all the vegetables. Fry the garlic and chili in the olive oil, and then add onions. When beginning to brown add the aubergine, courgettes and pepper. Keep stirring. Mix vegetable broth with tomato purée and pour over vegetables. Add sugar, pepper and cucumber. Cook very slowly until the excess liquid has gone. When the vegetables have become tender add the tomatoes. Let it cool, add vinaigrette sauce and serve.

TOMATO PURÉE

Put tomatoes into very hot water then peel the skins off. Mash the tomatoes and bring to boil until the consistency thickens and the taste become more concentrated. Add seasoning and brown sugar to taste.

Storing The Surplus Crops

Indoor farmers are far more likely to suffer shortages than gluts. But they do have the advantage that, provided the vegetables get sufficient light, perhaps boosted by artificial lamps in the gloomy months, the indoor conditions can mean all-year-round cropping. Storing for the lean days of winter may not be necessary.

But the knowledge of how to store is important for all home growers, not only if there is a chance, one day, of cultivating a larger outdoor area such as an allotment, but to be able to deal with any glut arising from a mess-up of the planning schedule, and the ripening of, say, all the tomatoes in the same week. It would be criminal not to store, thereby preventing decay, or at least give away such a surplus.

FREEZING

Deep freezing will preserve the taste, texture and nutritional value of your vegetables better than most other methods, although it is not necessarily the most economical way of going about it in the face of the ever-increasing cost of electricity. Most vegetables will freeze, with the exception of those that contain a great deal of water and are generally enjoyed raw. Don't try to freeze lettuce, cucumber, celery, tomatoes, onions, radishes, Jerusalem artichokes, aubergine or mushrooms.

In the seed catalogues you will often see references to varieties that are recommended for freezing. It is more important that you pick the varieties that are suitable for growing, in the limited space circumstances at your disposal, than worry about their freezability.

Freeze as soon after you pick your fruits and vegetables as possible, and only consider young, tender and unblemished specimens. Blanch them first in boiling water to de-activate the enzymes which might otherwise cause the vegetables to go off. Prepare them as if you were going to cook them, put into a wire blanching basket, and lower into the already boiling water. Start timing as soon as the water returns to the boil, and lift them out again according to the instructions that come with your freezer book (around two minutes, depending on the vegetable in question). Then plunge into cold water, or hold under the tap, for the same length of time. When they have cooled off, drain and pat dry with a cloth or kitchen roll paper. Pack into plastic bags or boxes and seal so that they remain airtight. You cannot re-freeze, so pack one serving per bag. Label, date and stick into the freezer.

With the exception of sweetcorn you do not have to thaw vegetables before cooking them. Since they have already been par-boiled you only need to cook them for about half their normal cooking time.

Soft fruits do not need to be bleached before packing, but wash well in cold water before doing so. They can also be frozen with sugar, or a sugar syrup, or frozen as juices, sauces or purées. Thaw out slowly, in a refrigerator, before eating.

DRYING

People did manage, somehow, to store their food in those grim days before freezers came along. You might prefer to store some fruits and vegetables, as well as herbs, by thoroughly drying them before packing away in jars, lidded tins, plastic lunch boxes and so on, and keeping them in a dry and darkish place until needed. Make a drying tray from an old picture frame, stretching and securing cheesecloth across one side, and standing on a trestle support. The ideal place for drying is where the temperature lies between 120 and 150 degrees fahrenheit, perhaps in an airing cupboard, near a radiator of in front of a fan heater.

Drying mushrooms is an excellent way to store a bumper crop, especially considering that they won't freeze. Slice them vertically, or thread on a string and hang up to dry. Beans retain their flavour well when dried, but they should be blanched for five minutes before storing. They can also be preserved by layering with salt in an earthenware pot.

PICKLES AND CHUTNEYS

Not only do these mean preservation for future consumption, they are also justified in their own right for the completely different sweet and sour taste and crispy texture that they produce.

Chutneys can be made from almost anything you are likely to grow, but courgettes and tomatoes take the prizes. Chop the vegetables finely and simmer for quite a while with a few raisins, some onion, ground pickling spices and sugar (brown, or use honey) in some vinegar. Once it has reduced to the consistency of thickish mud pour into clear jars and seal. Resist for a least two months.

Pickles should be made from firm-looking and feeling vegetables — green tomatoes, onions, garlic, peas, carrots, beets, cucumbers, radishes and so on. Wash and cut up, sprinkle with salt and let them stand overnight (leave onions to soak in brine). Mix the vinegar with whole pickling spices and herbs and boil for a few minutes in a pan. Rinse the salt off the vegetables, pat dry and put into jars (best to use those with a vacuum sealing lid). Pour the vinegar over them and seal. Filter, or decant the vinegar from the spices if you don't fancy a sludge at the bottom of the jars. Colder vinegar makes for crispier pickles.

This by no means exhausts the possibilities for storing home grown food. Try bottling tomatoes or fruits, storing roots in peat, making jams and juices, or your own fruity candies. Vegetables and fruits will make fine wines too.

Profit from your Produce

You are unlikely ever to succeed in earning a living from indoor farming. Your home would need to be of palatial proportions to provide sufficient resources, and if you could afford to live in such a grand manner it would make better sense to change your life style completely and buy a few acres of farmland.

But you could grow a surplus of one particular crop even on a small scale; indeed, if your planting schedules aren't well worked out beforehand you may find you have one on your hands despite any prior intentions. These extra crops could be stored, given away to friends and relatives, exchanged with the surplus crops of a neighbour, on a 'food co-op' barter system, or you could try to sell them to help recover some of your own growing costs.

Commercial producers, in the main, dispose of their produce through wholesale markets. You will only be able to compete with their low-cost, mass-marketing techniques by offering produce that is fresher, tastier or different, and preferably something that is grown organically without any chemical additives. The great appeal of your cash crop would be its home-grown quality, and a price that has not been upped by distribution and other merchandising costs.

Concentrate on what you think will appeal. It may be an unusual crop, such as salsify or Swiss chard, which is rarely seen in the local shops, or the mini varieties, such as tiny tomatoes or baby lettuces.

The potential market will be as varied as the place you live in. Try to get a Saturday stall at a market. Ask nearby restaurants and hotels if they would be interested in a small but regular supply of a gourmet variety. Local shopkeepers, especially health food stores, may agree to stock your supplies. Advertise in a local newspaper.

Don't be shy about asking because you won't find customers any other way. Pack your products to look attractive and use your imagination when it comes to fixing your prices — they'll have to be competitive, but the quality of your product may well command a premium price.

METRIC CONVERSION TABLES

Pints		Litres	Gallons		Litres
1.760	1	0.568	0.220	1	4.546
3.520	2	1.137	0.440	2	9.092
5.279	3	1.705	0.660	3	13.638
7.039	4	2.273	0.880	4	18.184
8.799	5	2.841	1.100	5	22.731
10.559	6	3.410	1.320	6	27.277
12.318	7	3.978	1.540	7	31.823
14.078	8	4.546	1.760	8	36.369
15.838	9	5.114	1.980	9	40.915

Ounces		Grams	Pounds		Kilograms
0.035	1	28.350	2.205	1	0.454
0.071	2	56.699	4.409	2	0.907
0.106	3	85.049	6.614	3	1.361
0.141	4	113.398	8.181	4	1.814
0.176	5	141.748	11.023	5	2.268
0.212	6	170.097	13.228	6	2.722
0.247	7	198.447	15.432	7	3.175
0.282	8	226.796	17.637	8	3.629
0.317	9	255.146	19.842	9	4.082

Inches		Millimetres	Feet		Metres
0.039	1	25.4	3.281	1	0.305
0.079	2	50.8	6.562	2	0.610
0.118	3	76.2	9.843	3	0.914
0.157	4	101.6	13.123	4	1.219
0.197	5	127.0	16.404	5	1.524
0.236	6	152.4	19.685	6	1.829
0.276	7	177.8	22.966	7	2.134
0.315	8	203.2	26.247	8	2.438
0.354	9	228.6	29.528	9	2.743

BIBLIOGRAPHY

George 'Doc' & Katy Abraham *Raise Vegetables Without A Garden* Countryside Books, Barrington Ill.,1974

Frank W. Allerton *Tomatoes For Everyone* Faber & Faber, London 1968

American Horticultural Society *Directory of American Horticulture* Rodale Press, Emmaus Pa. 1975

Anne Ashberry *Gardens On A Higher Level* Hodder & Stoughton, London 1969

F.C. Atkins *Mushroom Growing Today* Faber & Faber, London 1966

L.H. Bailey *Standard Cyclopedia of Horticulture* Macmillan 1914

Ed. Mitchell Beazley, George Seddon and Helena Radecka *Your Kitchen Garden* Mitchell Beazley, London 1975

J.K.A. Bleasdale *Plant Physiology In Relation To Horticulture* Macmillan, London 1973

E.D. Bickford and S. Dunn *Lighting for plant growth* Kent State University Press 1972

Arabella Boxer *Garden Cookbook* Weidenfeld & Nicolson, London 1974

H.E. Bravery & B.G. Furner *Home Made Wine-Making And Vine Growing* Macdonald, London 1973

William S. Brett & Kay Grant *Small City Gardens* Abelard-Schuman, New York 1967

British Agrochemicals Association *Directory of Garden Chemicals* 1976

Brooklyn Botanic Garden Handbook *Gardening Under Artificial Light* New York 1972

Dian Buchman *Feed Your Face* Duckworth, London 1973

J.D. Butler & N.F. Oebker *Hydroponics As A Hobby* Univ. of Illinois (Urbana-Champaign)

Anthony Byers *Growing Under Glass* Pelham, London 1974

A.E. Canham *A New Lamp For Daylength Control In Horticulture* British Electrical & Allied Industries Research Association, Leatherhead, Surrey 1962

A.E. Canham *Electricity in Horticulture* Macdonald, London 1964

A.E. Canham (Electrical Research Assoc.) Report: *Artificial Light In Horticulture* 1962

A.E. Canham *Artificial Light In Horticulture* Centrex, Eindhoven 1966

V.K. Chatterjee *Practice Of Soilless Cultivation* Alpha-Beta, Calcutta 1963

Elaine C. Cherry *Flourescent Light Gardening* D. Van Nostrand, Princeton, New Jersey 1965

James E. Churchill *The Homesteader's Handbook* Vintage Books, New York 1975

E.G. Coker *Horticultural Science & Soil* Macdonald, London 1971 (Vols. 1 & 2)

Consumers' Association *Extending Your House* 1971

Francis C. Coulter *A Manual of Home Vegetable Gardening* Dover, New York 1973

Thalassa Cruso *Making Things Grow* Michael Joseph, London 1969

Robert M. Devlin *Plant Physiology* Van Nostrand Reinhold, New York 1969

Alexandra & John Dickerman *Discovering Hydroponic Gardening* Woodbridge Press, Santa Barbara, Calif. 1975

Henry Doubleday Research Assoc/Lawrence D. Hills *Save Your Own Seed* Halstead Press

James Sholto Douglas *Beginner's Guide to Hydroponics* Drake, New York 1973

R.J. Downs & W.A. Bailey *Control of Illumination For Plant Growth* Thomas Y. Crowell Co., 1976

The Electricity Council *Growelectric Handbook No. 2 Lighting in Greenhouses* Sept. 1974

The Electricity Council *Growelectric Handbook No. 1 Growing Rooms* Oct. 1975

The Electricity Council *Growelectric Handbook No. 3 Ventilation for Greenhouses* Mar. 1975

Hazel Evans *Small Space Gardening*

J.R.B. Evison *Decorative Horticulture* Macdonald 1971

Xenia Field *Window Box Gardening* Blandford Press, London 1974

Louis N. Flawn *Tomato Growing For The Amateur* Foyle, London 1955

Louis N. Flawn *Profitable Gardening* C. Arthur Pearson, London 1961

L.N. & V.L. Flawn *The Cool Greenhouse All The Year Round* John Gifford, London 1966

L.N. & V.L. Flawn *Gardening Under Glass* John Gifford, London 1971

H.G. Witham Fogg *The Small Greenhouse* Arthur Barker 1967

Gertrude B. Foster *Herbs For Every Garden* J.M. Dent, London 1975

Mel Frank & Ed Rosenthal *Marijuana Grower's Guide* And/Or Press, San Francisco 1975

Brian Furner *The Kitchen Garden* Pan, London 1966

Alan Gemmell *The Penguin Book of Basic Gardening* Penguin, Harmondsworth 1975

Roy Genders *Mushroom Growing For Everyone* Faber & Faber, London 1969

Roy Genders *Gardening Indoors* Stanley Paul, London 1961

Gisela Gramenz *Indoor Gardens & Window Boxes* Lutterworth Press, London 1971

Adelma Grenier Simmons *Herbs To Grow Indoors* Hawthorn Books, New York 1969

Roger Grounds *Your Greenhouse* Ward Lock, London 1975

Zack Hanle *Cooking With Flowers* New English Library, London 1972

Cyril C. Harris & Marion Howells *Modern Ways of Growing and Cooking Vegetables* Pelham, London 1972

Cyril C. Harris *House Plants and Indoor Gardening* Octopus, London 1973

Dudley Harris *Hydroponics* David & Charles, Newton Abbot 1974

Walter Harter *Organic Gardening For City Dwellers* Warner Books, New York 1973

Dr. D.G. Hessayon *Be Your Own House Plant Expert* Pan Britannica, Herts.

Dr. D.G. Hessayon *Vegetable Plotter* Pan Britannica, Herts.

Dr. D.G. Hessayon *Be Your Own Gardening Expert* Pan Britannica, Herts.

Lawrence D. Hills *Pest Control Without Poisons* H.D.R.A., Braintree, Essex 1964

H.F. Hollis *Profitable Growing Without Soil* English Universities Press, London 1964

J.P. Hudson *Control of the plant environment* Butterworth Scientific Publications, London 1957

Humidity Advisory Service *Humidification*

Rich Israel & Reny Slay Home Steader's Handbook Grace 1973

J. Janick *Horticultural Science* W.H. Freeman & Co., San Francisco 1963

M.G. Kains *Five Acres and Independence* Dover, New York 1973

Bill Kaysing *First-time Farmer's Guide* Straight Arrow Books, San Francisco 1971

F.H. & J.L. Kranz *Gardening Indoors Under Lights* Viking Press, New York 1971

Louis C.C. Krieger *The Mushroom Handbook* Macmillan 1936

Richard W. Langer *Grow It* Avon Books, New York 1971

Claire Loewenfeld & Philippa Back *The Complete Book of Herbs & Spices* David & Charles, Newton Abbot 1974

Elvin McDonald *Gardening Under Lights* Popular Library, New York 1965

A.J. Macself *The Amateur's Greenhouse* Collingridge, London 1974

D.R. Matlin *Growing Plants Without Soil* Chemical Publishing Co. Inc., New York 1940

Ronald H. Menage *Woolman's Greenhouse Gardening* Hamish Hamilton 1974

Joan W. Meschter *HowTo Grow Herbs and Salad Greens Indoors* Popular Library, N.Y. 1975

Ministry of Agriculture *Asparagus* Bulletin 60 H.M.S.O. 1940

Ministry of Agriculture *Culinary and Medicinal Herbs* Bulletin 76 H.M.S.O. 1951

Ministry of Agriculture *Watercress Cultivation* Bulletin 135 H.M.S.O. 1956

Ministry of Agriculture, Fisheries & Food *The ABC of Preserving* H.M.S.O. 1969

H.J. Webb/Mist *Propagation and Automatic Watering* Faber & Faber, London 1970

Keith Mossman *The Garden Room* David & Charles, Newton Abbot 1973

Duane Newcomb *The Apartment Farmer* J.P. Tarcher, Los Angeles 1976

H. & W. Olkowski *The City People's Book of Raising Food*

Organic Gardening & Farming Monthly

Reader's Digest *Do-It-Yourself Manual*

A.R. Rees et.al. *Crop Processes in Controlled Environments* Academic Press London 1972

Tom Riker & Harvey Rottenberg *The Garderner's Catalogue-Food Gardens* Wm. Morrow , New York 1975

M.J. Rolls & R.B. Morrison *Science In the Garden* Blandford

T. Saunby *Soilless Culture* Collingridge, London 1953

Arthur J. Simons *The New Vegetable Grower's Handbook* Penguin, Harmondsworth 1975

Alice Skelsey *Farming In A Flowerpot* Workman Publishing Co., New York 1975

Violet Stevenson *Patio, Rooftop And Balcony Gardening* Collingridge, London 1967

Violet Stevenson *Indoor Gardening* Arthur Barker, London 1970

Meta Strandberg *Food Growing Without Poisons* Turnstone, London 1976

Editors of Sunset Books *Vegetable Gardening* Lane Books, Menlo Park, Calif. 1974

John Tampion *The Gardener's Practical Botany* David & Charles, Newton Abbot 1972

Homer C. Thompson & William C. Kelly *Vegetable Crops* McGraw Hill, New York 1957

United States Department of Agriculture *Complete Guide to Home Canning, Preserving and Freezing* Dover Publications, New York 1973

U.S. Dept. of Agriculture *Growing Plants Without Soil For Experimental Use (No. 1251)* Washington 1972

U.S. Dept. of Agriculture *Home and Garden Bulletin No. 187 Indoor Gardens With Controlled Lighting* 1971

U.S. Dept. of Agriculture *Light and Plants (No. 879)* Washington 1971

Brenda & Robert Vale *The Autonomous House* Thames & Hudson, London 1975

Ian Walls & A.S. Horsburgh *Making Your Garden Pay* David & Charles, Newton Abbot 1974

Ian Walls *Making the Most Of Your Greenhouse* Ward Lock, London 1975

Ian Walls *Simple Tomato Growing* Ward Lock, London 1975

Ian Walls *Tomato Growing Today* David & Charles, Newton Abbot 1972

F.W. Went *The Experimental Control of Plant Growth* Chronica Botanica Vol.17, Waltham Massachusetts 1957

Denis Wood & Kate Crosby *Grow It And Cook It* Faber & Faber, London 1975

R.C.M. Wright *Plant Propagation* Ward Lock, London 1955

Ed. Michael Wright *The Complete Indoor Gardener* Pan Books, London 1974

INDEX

Food for Free

RICHARD MABEY

Food for Free is an illustrated guide to the astonishing — and often delectable — range of wild British foods. Richard Mabey describes over 300 foods, including shellfish, fungi and seaweed, as well as edible roots and weeds, flowers and fruit. He discusses the nutritional and gastronomical value of each plant and gives guidance on how to find, gather and cook it.

Food for Free is a rich storehouse of anecdote, information and recipe, promising entertainment in the kitchen and ceaseless diversion on country walks.

'A superb and carefully compiled guide . . . the theme is that this island has an abundant store of free, wild food.' *Grimsby Evening Telegraph*

'Marjorie Blamey's illustrations are as delectable as the text. All in all, a book properly described as delicious.' *Sunday Times*

Large format. Fully illustrated.

Country Bazaar

ANDY PITTAWAY and BERNARD SCOFIELD

A handbook to country pleasures

Churning butter, tracking badgers,
Making rugs from home-dyed wool;
Finding clay and master-thatchers,
A spinning wheel or milking stool.

Throwing pots and pressing flowers,
Collecting honey and teasing yarn;
Making sun-dials tell the hours,
Keeping chickens in the barn.

Knots and sheep and goats and rambles,
Brasses, bees and animal spoor;
Baskets, trees and wayside brambles,
Smocks and shells and lots, lots more.

'This loving patchwork of crafts, folklore . . . has something for everybody.' *The Vegetarian*

'. . . a true rustic revel — innocent, sensual, joyous, gloriously chaotic, but with its feet always firmly on the earth.' Richard Mabey

'Glorious book of country pursuits, beautifully illustrated.' *Time Out*

Special large format. Lavishly illustrated throughout.

Not Just A Load of Old Lentils

ROSE ELLIOT

For the converted and the carniverous alike — a gourmet's guide to the best of vegetarian cookery.

Widely praised as one of the very best of vegetarian cookery books, Rose Elliot's 400 varied recipes will stimulate the converted to be more adventurous, and provide bored meat-eaters with a unique source of appetizing ideas — *Savoury Pie, Chinese Fried Rice, Courgette au Gratin, Mushroom Soufflé* and many more.

Combining a practical approach to the preparation of healthy meals with a dash of *haute cuisine*, these recipes banish once and for all the ogre of hard nut-cutlets and limp lettuce leaves.

' . . . a "must" on the kitchen shelf of those, not only vegetarians, who pride themselves on providing their families with meals of interest and variety.' *Span*

' . . . interesting and stimulating . . . recipes which cry out to be tried.' *Health for All*

' . . . a joy to use . . . ' *The Vegetarian*

A FONTANA SELECTION

Scotch Whisky

DAVID DAICHES

A colourful, affectionate and complete history of Scotch whisky from its early days as a cottage industry to the triumph of the great blending firms and the decline in popularity of the single malts in the present century. In his final chapters, he takes a connoisseur's look at the different qualities of individual malt whiskies; discriminating and knowledgeable, his one criterion is enjoyment.

Eat Fat and Grow Slim

RICHARD MACKARNESS

Richard Mackarness, a doctor and psychiatrist, presents a revolutionary and fully tested approach to slimming that encourages you to eat as much good food as you want while ignoring the calorie problem completely. How it works is clearly explained in the new and fully revised edition of this best-selling work, an immensely successful medically approved guide to the relationship between food and health.